THE **DAMN GOOD RESUME** GUIDE

THE
DAMN GOOD RESUME GUIDE

FIFTH EDITION

A CRASH COURSE IN RESUME WRITING

Yana Parker and Beth Brown

TEN SPEED PRESS
Berkeley

The authors wish to acknowledge their colleagues, friends, and clients, for their assistance, advice, and contributions to this project. Thank you, people!

Published in the United States by Ten Speed Press, an imprint of the Crown Publishing Group, a division of Random House, Inc., New York.
www.crownpublishing.com
www.tenspeed.com

Ten Speed Press and the Ten Speed Press colophon are registered trademarks of Random House, Inc.

Previous editions of the work were published in the United States by Ten Speed Press, Berkeley, in 1983, 1989, 1996, and 2002.

Library of Congress Cataloging-in-Publication Data

Parker, Yana.
  The damn good resume guide : a crash course in resume writing / Yana Parker and Beth Brown. — 5th ed.
    p. cm.
  Includes index.
  1. Résumés (Employment) I. Brown, Beth, 1959– II. Title.
  HF5383.P35 2012
  650.14'2—dc23
                                    2012004816
ISBN 978-1-60774-265-4
eISBN 978-1-60774-266-1

Printed in the United States of America

Design by Betsy Stromberg

10 9 8 7 6 5 4 3 2 1

Fifth Edition

CONTENTS

HOW I CAME TO WRITE
THE DAMN GOOD RESUME GUIDE

LONG-TIME INTEREST

For many years I've had a great interest in people's work lives and job satisfaction (including my own); this first showed up in a three-year volunteer job as director and coordinator of a community youth employment service. That led to a job with an upstate New York community college project to train unemployed high-school dropouts in job-related skills, and then on to a similar position as "Community Worker" with New York state employment offices in Albany, Troy, and Schenectady— a job I really loved.

Later, living in California, I noticed that many of the people in my personal network were involved in career counseling and small business development, so I started organizing get-togethers to brainstorm and strategize about our own work, just for the fun of it. Then, in 1979, I decided to try self-employment, using my writing skills and my new red-hot IBM Selectric typewriter. I resigned from office work in the big city to use my talents in a more personally rewarding way. I began by offering an editing, typing, and business-writing service out of my home in Oakland, but soon specialized in resumes, because it turned out to be a natural for me, and because very few people seemed to know how to do it well.

THE HUMBLE FREEBIE GETS STATUS

I never really set out to write or publish this book. It started out, in 1980, as just a few loose pages of instructions and examples, handed to clients as "homework" before we'd get together to work on their resume. (I'd grown weary of giving the same instructions verbally over and over, so I'd finally written them down.)

In our "Briarpatch" self-help group of small-business people, there was a financial consultant, Roger Pritchard, and one day I hired him to help me look critically at the fragile economics of my business. He noticed the packet of "homework" pages I gave to clients (by now it included sample resumes and a list of action verbs), and he asked, "Why are you giving this away? Don't you see that it's valuable, and that you could easily get a few dollars for it?"

So I took his advice and at the same time expanded the packet and wrote up the instructions in greater detail. I designed a card-stock cover, stapled everything together, and priced it at $2. Over the following year I expanded it twice more, the cover price increased, and I began to suspect that it might be marketable as a how-to guide independent of my resume writing business. So I typed it up even more carefully, added some graphics, designed a more professional cover, and persuaded two Berkeley bookstores to carry a few copies on consignment.

GETTING PUBLISHED

It turned out that Phil Wood, owner of Ten Speed Press, almost immediately found a copy in Cody's Bookstore, liked it, and proposed publishing it.

Now, many years and multiple revisions later, *The Damn Good Resume Guide* has clearly become respected and very popular in its field, with well over half a million copies in print. Professional job counselors call it "the best available," and a fair number of job clubs and career development centers (and even college instructors in business writing, psychology, and women's studies!) use *The Damn Good Resume Guide* as required reading.

—Yana Parker

IN YANA'S FOOTSTEPS—REVISING
THE DAMN GOOD RESUME GUIDE

Since Yana first pioneered the idea of a resume as a marketing tool, times have changed. We are now moving rapidly through the twenty-first century—and barely able to keep up with ourselves, in many ways. In the world of job hunting and resume writing, some things have changed, while others have remained the same. It's still important to create a document that is clear, accurate, articulate, and easy to read. It's still crucial that job seekers highlight their experience and accomplishments in a way that is relevant to the prospective employer, and it's still crystal clear that many people need help with marketing themselves and their skills to get a job that meets their needs. Now, however, there are many more ways available to create, deliver, and distribute resumes to the outside world, due to the explosion of the World Wide Web and the ever-expanding assortment of online marketing tools.

I've been "walking in Yana's footsteps" for more than fifteen years, writing resumes, cover letters, and other materials to help job seekers navigate the ever-changing job search landscape. As a "bridge builder," I have worked with people from all over the world—corporate, nonprofit, public sector, military to civilian, career changers, executives, college grads, fifty-plus, public figures, parents and others reentering the work force, white collar, blue collar, and green collar! As it was for Yana, resume writing was a natural for me, and I've enjoyed finding ways to support, empower, and build the confidence of every job seeker, with the same sense of humor and the same straightforward, no-nonsense compassion that Yana was known for.

During my training to become a resume writer in 1995, I had lunch with Yana. We talked about many things, including but not limited to resume writing. I was glad to meet her and appreciated her warmth, humor, and clarity. For the next several years, I contributed to Yana's *Damn Good* newsletter.

Yana herself was always keeping up with trends and ideas; she would readily change her opinion and/or attitude about job-related subjects and publish her latest findings and thinking in her monthly newsletters. Although some things have remained the same in the job search world, there are now distinct differences, particularly related to the *digital age*. In the *digital world* what has changed is *how* resumes are being read. This revised and updated book provides readers with tools to help quell their fears of technology, while also providing access to up-to-date information about the latest in resumes, cover letters, and other job search tools via the companion website, www.damngood.com.

It has been an honor (and great fun!) to update *The Damn Good Resume Guide* to bring it more fully into the twenty-first century.

—Beth Brown

SPECIAL THANKS

Special thanks to Richard Bolles for his invaluable help with Yana's original book.

WHAT'S NEW IN THIS EDITION

Many of the features of earlier editions of *The Damn Good Resume Guide* are still included here, such as the Action Verbs list, Informational Interviewing, and Cover Letters. *This* edition also has some important new features:

- Revised and updated Ten Steps, including how to "polish and proof" your resume

- Introducing: the Hybrid or Combination resume format

- New and updated sample resumes and cover letters . . . and cover *emails*

- New appendices, including Customizing Your Resume and Social Networking

TEN STEPS TO WRITING A GREAT RESUME

Here's a brief summary of the ten steps to writing a great resume:

STEP 1 Choose a job objective (also called a target job or career objective).

STEP 2 Find out what skills, knowledge, and experience are needed to do that target job.

STEP 3 Choose a resume format that fits your situation—chronological, functional, or a hybrid of the two.

STEP 4 Make a list of past jobs you've held, in chronological order.

STEP 5 For each job you've held, list your skills and accomplishments that show your knowledge or expertise.

STEP 6 Describe each accomplishment in a simple, powerful action statement that emphasizes the results that benefited your employer.

STEP 7 Arrange your action statements according to the format you chose in Step 3.

STEP 8 List your education, training, and any professional development that is relevant to your target job.

STEP 9 Summarize your key points at or near the top of the resume.

STEP 10 Polish and proof—review the whole document and make it shine!

(Note: In real-life resume writing, we do skip around. *So don't worry if YOUR resume comes together in some other sequence . . . as long as you do Step 1 and Step 2 first!*)

USEFUL DEFINITIONS

To help us start off on the right foot, here are some definitions of terms that will be used throughout this book:

A **"DAMN GOOD" RESUME** is a self-marketing tool—a kind of personal advertisement—that shows off your job skills and their value to a future (also called "prospective") employer. The main **purpose** of a resume is to **help you get a job interview.** So it starts off by naming your job objective and then describes your skills, experience, and accomplishments as they relate to THAT job objective.

Remember, writing a good resume is *very different* from filling out a job application. An application form is about JOBS and gives just the facts of your employment history. But a "DAMN GOOD" resume is about YOU and how you perform in your jobs. *It's very important to see the difference!*

A **CHRONOLOGICAL RESUME** presents your work experience in a traditional, **by-date** format, listing the jobs you've held and describing the activities and accomplishments of each job in separate statements, also called **bullet points,** with the **most recent job appearing first.**

A **FUNCTIONAL RESUME** presents your work experience by listing the most important **skill areas** you've used, and then describing a number of your accomplishments and activities (drawn from ALL of your jobs and life experiences) to illustrate those skills.

A **HYBRID (or COMBINATION) RESUME** lists your work experience in the same **by-date format** as the chronological resume, but then, within the most recent job you've held, it organizes and presents your accomplishments **within the skill areas that are relevant to your future job.** It's like a functional resume INSIDE of a chronological resume!

NOTE: A Damn Good Resume can be chronological, functional, or a hybrid of the two, because regardless of the format, it focuses on a clear job objective and then emphasizes your work/life accomplishments to clearly show your unique value to an employer. In Step 3, we'll talk more about each format, to help you make the best decision for YOUR resume.

ONWARD TO THE TEN STEPS!

On the following pages you'll find that each of the ten steps is first explained in detail, and then is followed by "Yes, but's"—some of the problems and dilemmas you may face as you do that step. When the "Yes, but" sounds like YOUR problem, then follow the directions to resolve it. But if you have no difficulty completing a particular step, IGNORE the corresponding "Yes, but" and move straight ahead to the next step. Got it? Okay, let's GO!

>>> ► **HOT TIP**

The process of creating your new resume has other great benefits: By articulating what is valuable about your skills and experience, building your new resume can help you **prepare for a job interview** and even help you **negotiate your salary!**

A CRASH COURSE IN RESUME WRITING

(You can do Steps 3 through 10 in any order, but be SURE to do Step 1 and Step 2 FIRST.)

STEP 1

Choose a job objective

(also called a *career objective*, *target job*, *career goal*, or simply *objective*).

For some people, this can be the hardest step. But it is also the most important! Remember, your resume is your *self-marketing tool*—that means that you are marketing YOU. Your resume needs to be FOCUSED on your target audience; that is, the prospective employer who will read your resume and call you in for an interview.

So, stating a clear job objective will help you, in two big ways:

1. It will **tell a prospective employer** "This is the job I want." The rest of your resume will show the employer why you are an **ideal candidate** for that job.

2. It will **help YOU focus your attention on your goal.** That way, it will be easier for you to decide what to include in your resume and what to leave out, what to emphasize and what to downplay.

Now, I know that some of you might be thinking, "I've seen job objective statements that are vague and go on and on and on. For example: 'Seeking a challenging position in which I can use my extensive skills and experience to meet the challenges.' How is that going to help me get a job?"

You're right! That kind of job objective statement is not helpful at all; in fact, it's BORING! The best job objectives are the most SPECIFIC and BRIEF. For example:

Job Objective: **Merchandising Manager for Levi Strauss**

YES, BUT . . . "I am really not sure what sort of job I want; I just need a job!"

If you are not sure what type of job you want:

- **Make a list of your strongest and most favorite skills** (start out with three or four skills) that you would like to use in your new job.
- **Find out what jobs or career areas call for those skills and abilities.**
- **Choose one of those jobs as your current job objective.**

Getting clear about your job direction is CRUCIAL, and it's not as impossible as you might think. It requires using both your "left brain"—the side that's analytical and goes step-by-step toward a goal—and your "right brain"—the side that gets an intuitive "hunch" or just "knows" when something feels right for you. You'll have to take a little time to do some exploring and maybe some research, and also think about what you'd really LIKE to do and CAN do.

Here are a few ways to get help with this part of the process:

1. **Seek help from a professional career counselor or coach.** These specialists can work with you to identify your skills and offer ways to help you choose a career path or next job objective.

2. **Check out search engines** like Google to do **online research** about your interests and the possible jobs they could be a good match for.

3. **Use your social network to get more information.** Now that we are in the digital age, we have a lot of resources at our fingertips. Many people are members of social networks, such as Facebook and Twitter, as well as professional networks such as LinkedIn. These networks can be helpful, because they give you access to many people who might know something about the industry, field, company, career path, organization, or position you are interested in. (See **Appendix C** for more information on **social networking**.)

4. Once you have made a connection or two with people in the field or job you are interested in, **try out informational interviewing** to get more of a feeling for the type of position, field, or industry you are exploring. (We'll talk about **informational interviewing** in more detail in **Appendix B**.)

(I can hear you muttering: "Don't do this to me—I don't have TIME for this stuff." But without a clear focus on your goal, you can spin in circles endlessly. Taking the time to get FOCUSED pays off by helping you get the job you want!)

YES, BUT . . . "I want to explore several possibilities. Can't I just write a 'generic' resume?"

If you want to explore more than one type of job, you will need more than one resume. (Please, no groaning—it can be fun!) This is also where the job objective can help you. Whenever you change your job objective, it can help you change or reorganize the information in the rest of the resume so that you are once again a great candidate for a job that you want. (Check out **Appendix D** to learn about **customizing your resume** for different job opportunities.)

Remember, when it comes to resumes, there is no such thing as "generic"! Some people just write down everything they've ever done, in the hope that the prospective employer will take the time to figure out what type of job they should be hired for. Well, most employers don't have that kind of time, or interest. They want people who know what they want.

STEP 2

Find out what skills, knowledge, and experience are needed to do that target job.

(These are sometimes called *KSAs*, or *"Knowledge, Skills, and Abilities."*)

This step is as crucial as Step 1, because if you don't know what's needed, you won't know what to emphasize and what to leave out. So your resume will not do a good job of selling you to a prospective employer, who is looking for people who KNOW the requirements of the job.

YES, BUT . . . "I'm not sure if I even want that job; also, I don't have ANY idea how to get that information, short of HAVING the job in the first place!"

Now that we have entered the twenty-first century (well, most of us have!), there are many ways to find out information about the KSAs for specific jobs, fields, industries, companies, organizations, and government agencies. You may have already used some of the following ways in Step 1 to get focused on your job objective (and it may have also helped you feel more comfortable with new ways of doing research). Now you can use the tools listed below to home in on the details of what you'll need to prepare a *focused and effective* resume.

- Use the World Wide Web to do **online research** about a particular position, company, or industry. For example, using Google or another search engine, enter the company name or the industry and your desired city and state. Take a look at the different websites that come up and print out the information or write down the job descriptions of positions that sound interesting to you. Or you can go to a few different websites for your target industry, or for a specific company, organization, or government agency. These sites often list job opportunities that you can read about and see what "clicks" for you.

The main reason why people don't write effective resumes is that they trip over Steps 1, 2, and 6; that is . . .

- **They don't choose a clear job objective (Step 1), or they don't find out what's required in the new job (Step 2).** Already they're off to a bad start!

- **They describe all of their past jobs** by reciting the **official job descriptions** (b-o-r-i-n-g) **instead of vividly describing what they accomplished** in those jobs or how they made themselves valuable to their employers by producing good results. This is where powerful action statements (Step 6) become essential.

Another reason people don't write great resumes is that **they forget what a resume really is!** So check out the USEFUL DEFINITIONS on page 2.

- Use **social networking** tools such as LinkedIn, Facebook, and Twitter to reach professionals in the fields or positions you are interested in. Ask them to give you a quick, five-point overview of the qualifications needed for the job you are seeking. (See **Appendix C** for more information about **social networking**.)

- Once you find a job listing that sounds like a good fit for you, use the job listing as your guide. Highlight key words and phrases that describe the level and type of experience, special skills, personality traits, training, and education required *or preferred* by the employer.

- In addition to using the Internet—or if you don't have Internet access—check out the classified ads in your local newspaper. You can also go to the *Dictionary of Occupational Titles* (D.O.T.), found at your local library or employment office, and take notes about the KSAs needed for jobs that seem exciting to you.

- Ask someone in your personal or professional network to connect you with someone who already has a similar position or does the same kind of work, then contact him or her for an **informational interview** (as described in **Appendix B**).

Whatever method or methods you decide to use, **make a list** of the most important qualifications needed to do your target job.

― STEP **3** ―

Choose a resume format that fits your situation—chronological, functional, or a hybrid of the two.

There are three main ways to format your resume: chronological, functional, and hybrid. Let's talk about each one briefly:

The **CHRONOLOGICAL** format presents your work experience in a more traditional way, listing your jobs in reverse chronological order, with the most recent job first, and describing your achievements under each job title.

Job Title #1 (most recent job)
- Something I accomplished in that job
- Something else I accomplished in that job

Job Title #2 (previous job)
- Something I accomplished in that job
- Something else I accomplished in that job

Job Title #3 (the job before that)
- Something I accomplished in that job
- Something else I accomplished in that job

The **FUNCTIONAL** format presents your work experience by emphasizing the SKILLS involved, creating *skill headings* (also called *skill areas* or *skill sets*), and grouping your achievements (drawn from ALL of your jobs and life experiences) under the appropriate skill heading. Your "bare bones" chronological list of jobs goes AFTER the skill sets, at or near the end of your resume.

Relevant Skill #1—most relevant to target job
- Something I've accomplished using that skill
- Something else I've accomplished using that skill

Relevant Skill #2—next most important/relevant
- Something I've accomplished using that skill
- Something else I've accomplished using that skill

Relevant Skill #3—next most important/relevant
- Something I've accomplished using that skill
- Something else I've accomplished using that skill

Job Title #1

Job Title #2

Job Title #3

The **HYBRID** (also known as **COMBINATION**) resume might be considered the best of both worlds, because it is a combination of the chronological and functional resume formats, and it can accomplish what neither of them can do alone: it can show your accomplishments within skill sets *inside of* the chronological format.

Job Title #1 (most recent)

Relevant Skill #1
- Something I've accomplished using that skill
- Something else I've accomplished using that skill

Relevant Skill #2
- Something I've accomplished using that skill
- Something else I've accomplished using that skill

Relevant Skill #3
- Something I've accomplished using that skill
- Something else I've accomplished using that skill

Job Title #2 (previous job)
- Something I accomplished in that job
- Something else I accomplished in that job

Job Title #3 (the job before that)
- Something I accomplished in that job
- Something else I accomplished in that job

To keep your resume an appropriate length, you can use the hybrid format for your most recent job or for the job you held for the longest time, and then use the regular chronological format for your other jobs within the same resume.

YES, BUT . . . "I can't decide which format to choose and it's driving me crazy!"

Don't worry—any format can work if it's done well. Here are a few pointers to help you determine which resume format will work best for you.

It's best to use the chronological format if:

- You are staying in the same field and "moving up the ladder" in responsibility or level.

- You have an unbroken employment history (no gaps).

- You know that the prospective employer prefers the chronological format or is more conservative (such as in the technology or financial services industries).

It's best to use the functional format if:

- You are changing careers.

- You have gaps in your employment history, and you have life experience and skills relevant to your target job.

- Your relevant skills—those required for your new job objective—are not obvious when someone sees only your chronological work history.

- You know that the prospective employer prefers the functional format, or is open to it, such as positions in the social services or nonprofit sector.

It's best to use the hybrid or combination format if:

- You have been at one job for a long time and have worn many hats—that is, you have had multiple responsibilities and have used many different skills to get the job done.

- You know that the prospective employer prefers the chronological format, but your relevant skills are not as obvious in that format, so you want to highlight them within your chronological work history to help the reader see that you have the skills necessary to do your target job.

STEP 4

Make a list of past jobs you've held, in chronological order.

No matter which format you choose, you will still need to show your work history somewhere on your resume, in chronological order. This can include both paid and unpaid work (WORK is WORK is WORK!), as well as schooling, volunteer activities, and so on.

Start by listing your most recent job first, then your earlier jobs. Give the dates of employment, your job title or titles, and the employer or company name, city, and state. Remember to include any unpaid work or education that will fill a gap or that shows you have the skills for the job.

>>> **HOT TIP**

For each of your jobs, you can list just the *years* of employment, not the months. This will eliminate short-term gaps and give your work history a more seamless look.

Here's how it might look:

2009–present	**Executive Assistant to the CEO**	Berringer & Berringer, New York, NY
2007–2008	**Administrative Assistant**	Peterson Electric Co., Teaneck, NJ
2004–2007	**Receptionist**	G. B. Franklin & Sons, Paterson, NJ

Here's an example from a recent college grad interested in a career in marketing:

2011–present	**Marketing Manager**	Macy's, San Francisco, CA
2010	**Marketing Assistant**	Macy's, San Francisco, CA
2006–2010	**Full-time Student, Marketing**	California State University, Hayward, CA

And another example, from a job hunter who moved up at the same company over the years:

2000–present	**AT&T, Inc.,** San Bruno, CA	
	Customer Service Representative	2006–present
	Telephone Repair Supervisor	2003–2006
	Line Repairman	2000–2003

Here's an excerpt from the resume of a mom returning to work, preferably in photography:

2007–2012	**Full-time Parent**	Chicago, IL
2005–2007	**Staff Photographer**	Triangle, Inc., Catalog Department, Evansville, IN
2002–2004	**Photojournalist**	*The Evansville Times,* Evansville, IN

And lastly, a job seeker recently in transition from the military to a civilian position:

2010–present	**Operations Manager**	Solutions to Moving, Inc., Corporate Relocation Services, New Orleans, LA
2001–2010	**Lieutenant Colonel**	United States Air Force
	Chief, Inspector General, USAF Air Transportation	2007–2010
	Deputy Director, USAF Cargo & Requirements	2006–2007
	Assistant Deputy Director, Cargo Operations	2001–2006

 YES, BUT . . . "This is really tough for me. For one thing, I have a lot of little gaps (and one big one) in my work history. Also, I don't know if I should list EVERYTHING—I'll look like a job-hopper or a flake, with all those short-term jobs! Besides, some of those jobs I'd like to *forget*, they're so unimpressive."

 Initially, just to create an overview for yourself, list ALL your past jobs; then check the following list for what to leave in, what to leave out, and what to modify.

What to Include on Your New Resume

- **Include ALL of your jobs,** however short-term they were, *if* you are very young or you have very little work experience.

- **Include ALL of the jobs that show experience related to your job objective,** even if they were short-term or unpaid.

- **Include jobs that are not particularly related to your current job goal** *if* they help create a picture of stability—but don't describe them in detail.

- **Include unpaid work** *if* it helps prove you have pertinent skills and experience, or *if* it fills in a gap. (See examples on pages 11 and 12.)

- You can also **include a period of training or education** in your work history *if* it is related to your job goal, or *if* it helps fill in a gap, as shown on pages 20, 21, and 28.

What to Leave Out of Your New Resume

- **Omit jobs that were very brief** *unless* they are needed to show how you developed your skills, or to fill in a skimpy work history. Remember to round off your employment dates to years, to eliminate small gaps (of up to one year).

- **Omit** your earliest jobs if you're worried about age discrimination. You can assume that most employers are interested in only the past ten years of your work history, unless you know or find out otherwise.

- You can also **omit jobs that aren't important to your new job objective**—or jobs that you disliked or that create a not-so-great impression—as long as dropping them doesn't leave a big hole in your work history. If you have to include them, just keep your description short and simple.

If you've had only odd jobs, short-term work, or self-employment, there are several ways to deal with this, depending on your situation:

- If you did roughly the same kind of odd job repeatedly, or for a long period of time, you can **create your own job title,** such as "Freelance," "Consultant," or "Self-employed." For example:

Household Repairman (self-employed), Chicago, IL, 2007–present
Interior Design Consultant, Boston, MA, 2007–present
Freelance Photographer, Detroit, MI, 2007–present

Because these jobs can't be verified through the normal channels, it will be very important to **find a few people you have worked for who can act as good references.** In this case, you may also need to add a line to the bottom of your resume, such as "Client references available upon request"—or, in the case of the photographer, "Portfolio available upon request."

- **If you've done lots of very different odd jobs,** it may be more of a challenge to list your work experience in a way that shows the employer you are stable, focused, and hard-working, but the basic idea is the same: **create an appropriate job title** (or titles) and list it just like a regular job. You should pick the odd jobs that you did most often and are most relevant to your target job, and ignore the others, for simplicity and to make a better impression. Again, don't mention any demeaning jobs or jobs you hated, if you can possibly leave them out. For example:

Home improvement projects, New Orleans, LA, 2007–present

- **If you've been self-employed for quite a while,** then your work history can't be easily verified by just one phone call. But you can still prove to a new employer that you really DO have the experience, and also a record of reliability, by **detailing specific projects and results** and by providing good letters of recommendation from past clients and customers. For example:

Computer software consultant, Washington, DC, 2006–present
Selected clients include: Kramer, Larsen & Bing
                             Wiser Leiner, Inc.
                             Paradigm Graphics

If you've only worked through temporary agencies, you can handle that gracefully by listing the temp agency (or agencies) as the EMPLOYER on your resume, and pick the job title that covers most of the temp work you did. Then, under that, you can list the specific assignments, describing your accomplishments, experience, and the skills you gained. **Round off dates.** It could look like this:

> **>>> HOT TIP**
>
> Except for the special cases described on this page, you don't need to automatically put "References available upon request" on your resume, as it just takes up valuable space. However, if an employer asks you for references at your interview, you should have a list of references ready. Usually, two to four references are needed, including the name, job title, company, city, state, phone, and email of each person. (*See examples of reference pages at www.damngood.com.*)

| 2008–present | **Administrative Assistant/Secretary** |
| | Kelly Services, Atlanta, GA |

Assignments and Accomplishments:

- Assisted senior managers with calendaring, correspondence, and special projects at diverse businesses in the greater Atlanta area.
- Conducted accurate year-end inventory for graphic design studio.
- Answered busy phones and greeted clients for two downtown law firms.

If you have a gap in your work history due to unemployment, here are some ways to handle that:

- If you are CURRENTLY unemployed, it will help a LOT to **find an immediate, short-term opportunity to get some unpaid/volunteer work experience,** preferably in your desired line of work, or paid work through a temporary agency, and **put that on your resume now,** even if you don't start until next week. This will look better on your resume than being unemployed. (If you list unpaid or volunteer work, rename the section heading to read "Work History" or "Experience," rather than "Employment History" or "Professional Experience.")

- For any PREVIOUS periods of unemployment, think back to what you were actually doing. If you can find ANYTHING that could be presented as "work," then create a job title for it that will have credibility in the work world. Be realistic; at the same time, **don't buy into the idea that certain work "doesn't count." Instead, present that work with dignity.** This includes taking time out for **full-time parenting** (which is really a more-than-full-time job!). Here are some examples from several different resumes:

2010–present	Full-time Caregiver—home care of elderly parent, Mobile, AL
2007–2009	Electronics Trainee, City College, San Francisco, CA
2006–2007	Apprentice Painter, Moe's Paint Shop, Boulder, CO
2006	Self-employed Repairman, Springfield, IL
2008–2010	Full-time Graduate Student, Mills College, Oakland, CA
Spring 2005	Board Member and Event Committee Chair
	Winfield High School, Winfield, MO
2004–2008	Full-time Parent and Girl Scout Leader, Wilmington, DE

For each job you've held, list your skills and accomplishments that show your knowledge or expertise.

Here's where the fun really starts! You've got your job objective; you've found out the skills, knowledge, and experience needed for that target job; you've chosen your resume format; and you've written out your work history, in reverse chronological order. Remember, "work history" in this case means ANY WORK you've done—paid, volunteer, parenting, hobbies, *whatever*—that refined the skills and knowledge you need for your desired new job.

Now it's time to think about and write down the SKILLS YOU HAVE that match the requirements of the job you want, and then to write down your ACCOMPLISHMENTS that illustrate that skill.

YES, BUT . . . "I don't know what my skills *are*! In a way, I'm good at a *lot* of different things, so how do I know what skills to put on my resume?"

Of course you have lots of skills and abilities, but not ALL of them necessarily belong on your resume. Go back to Step 2 and see what skills are REQUIRED for your target job. Ideally, you have *some* or *all* of those skills, and *those* are the skills that belong on *this* resume. You may not have all of the skills or experience needed, but don't give up; you could be selected for the job anyway, if you have enough of the basics under your belt, and appear to be able to quickly LEARN the remaining skills needed.

> **》》➤ HOT TIP**
>
> Don't forget your family, friends, work colleagues, and teachers—they are all part of your SOCIAL NETWORK—and they may have some valuable insights regarding your skills, as well as JOB OPPORTUNITIES that are out there that might be perfect for you.

If you identify many more skills than are required (or "preferred") for the job—and you probably will!—resist the urge to put them all on your resume. You may be a great quilter or skateboarder or sailor, but those skills **may not be at all relevant to your job objective,** and relevance is the main criterion for what DOES and DOES NOT belong on your new resume.

Also, **informational interviewing** (described in **Appendix B**) comes in very handy here; somebody who is in a similar job already is in a great position to tell you what skills are needed or useful in any particular position, industry, or field.

The following are some examples of how to write down the skills and accomplishments that are relevant to your target job. Don't worry about getting it all down "perfectly" right now. You're brainstorming here—just putting it all down on paper to see what you've got. The accomplishment statements that follow are still in the form of notes—in Step 6, we'll refine them and turn them into powerful action statements:

Job Objective: Position as a Pharmaceutical Sales Representative
Relevant Skills: Sales
Customer Service/Client Relationships
Knowledge of Medical Terminology

Key Accomplishments:

- I set a sales record by increasing average monthly sales from $3,000 to $15,000 selling portable exercise equipment, surpassing all of my other team members for any given month in the company's history.
- I built solid relationships with key decision-makers throughout my territory, and expanded the Western territory by 25 percent within my first six months on the job.
- I consulted with physicians, nurses, personal trainers, chiropractors, and massage therapists, using my knowledge of medical terminology to forge strong relationships and make sure they were satisfied with our products.

Job Objective: Position in Merchandising Display
Relevant Skills: Merchandising
Creativity/Design
Problem-Solving

Key Accomplishments:

- As a freelance photographer, I set up creative and lively photo shoots that resulted in a significant number of repeat and referral customers.
- I designed my own marketing materials that attracted customers from previously untapped areas, such as teenagers and executive business professionals.
- I monitored my inventory and reordered materials and supplies as needed to keep up with business volume.

Job Objective: Position in Employment Services
Relevant Skills: Research
Networking and Coordination
Technical/Computer skills

Key Accomplishments:

- I conducted extensive research on current job resources, materials, and market trends.
- I matched business executives with job seekers in related fields to facilitate the process of setting up informational interviews.
- I instituted an online Job Information Bulletin Board for career search networking.

>>> ► HOT TIP

Another way to identify the skills and experience you will need for your target job is to study the JOB LISTING for the job you want. (Download and print it out if you found it online.) Then, as in Step 2, grab that pencil, pen, or yellow highlighter and **circle or highlight the key skills** that you find in the job listing. Use them as your jumping-off point to help you think about which of your skills and accomplishments show that you have what the job listing is looking for.

YES, BUT . . . "I can't think of any accomplishments—and anyway, I'm not exactly sure what you mean by accomplishments."

We asked Rhonda Findling, a vocational rehabilitation counselor, how to approach this problem; her suggestions are listed below.

1. Learn to recognize your accomplishments. They are *very* important if you want your resume to stand out. Even if you don't have *measurable* accomplishments to put on your resume (such as "Increased sales 40%"), try to recall any **evidence of accomplishments** you may have overlooked.

   For example, you might include recognition from a variety of sources, such as:

   - **Being asked by your employer or direct supervisor to take on more responsibility:**
     - Chosen from a staff of 15 to train new employees in the children's clothing department.
     - Selected by manager to handle special and rush assignments.
   - **Being awarded an advancement or promotion:**
     - Promoted to senior cargo handler in 2008.
     - Promoted three times in two years, based on outstanding performance and leadership.
   - **Earning a bonus** for bringing in a new account, resolving a major issue, or handling a difficult customer.
   - **Getting good feedback on performance evaluations.** You can transform those positive comments into accomplishment statements.
   - **Receiving recognition from other sources,** such as customers, coworkers, outside agencies, union leaders, even competitors.

   Here's an example from a flight attendant's resume:

   - Received more than 100 personal letters of gratitude from passengers served over a 12-year period.

2. Discover some accomplishments through the "P.A.R." approach, looking at the things you did on the job in terms of **problems, actions, and results.** (This is one of my favorite resume techniques.) Ask yourself the following questions and write down your answers:
   - What PROBLEM existed in your workplace?
   - What ACTION did you take to resolve the problem?
   - What were the beneficial RESULTS of your action?

> **HOT TIP**
>
> Having a lot of **specialized knowledge** in your field (for example, the Knowledge of Medical Terminology on page 14) can be considered the same as a "relevant skill" for this purpose. See additional examples of accomplishment statements in the Sample Resumes section of this book, and also on the "damn good" website, www.damngood.com.

Here are a few examples:

- Transformed a disorganized, inefficient warehouse into a smooth-running operation by completely redesigning the layout, saving the company $250,000 in recovered stock.
- Thoroughly audited billing records and persevered in telephone collection follow-up, collecting thousands of dollars in overdue or unbilled fees.
- Successfully avoided the loss of over $1M in potential business failure of primary contractor by negotiating directly with subcontractors.

P.A.R. statements are powerful because they show clear examples of your delivering results for your current or previous employer, directly or indirectly. This should look very interesting to your potential new employer.

3. Talk to yourself! If you can't think of anything great to say about yourself or the things you've accomplished, **ask yourself the following questions.** This may get your creative juices flowing.

- Do my coworkers or my boss always count on me for certain things they know I'm good at? **What, specifically, do they think I'm good at?**
- If my friends at work were to brag about me to somebody else, what would they brag about? What does that say about my skills?
- If I had to teach a new employee the tricks of the trade—that is, teach them how to do a GREAT job in my line of work—**what do I do that's special, that I could teach this new employee?**
- If I suddenly had to leave the area—say, to take care of a sick relative—**what would my work buddies miss about me** while I was away? How would their jobs be tougher when I wasn't there to help?
- If I had to put together a training manual for my job (or for the job I'm looking for), **how would I describe what it takes to do this job superbly?**

STEP 6

Describe each accomplishment in a simple, powerful action statement that emphasizes results that benefited your employer.

>>> **HOT TIP**

DON'T mention activities you never want to do again—or you may end up with a job you don't enjoy!

You've already seen some accomplishment or action statements in Step 5, and you've done some brainstorming about your own achievements. Now here are a few pointers to make those action statements STRONG:

- Keep the language of your resume lively. Avoid tired, overused words and phrases. Instead of "Responsible for . . ." or "Responsibilities include . . ." (BORING!), start each statement with an **action verb.**

- Watch out for redundancy; that is, start each point with a **different** verb (not just "Managed" or "Developed") and don't repeat yourself, even if you've done the same basic things at more than one of your jobs. Figure out a new way of stating each accomplishment, or approach it from a different angle. (See **Appendix A** for a list of **action verbs** to help jump-start your action statements.)

- Be specific, paint a picture, and quantify results wherever possible.

- Resumes don't usually include the use of **personal pronouns** such as "I" or "my"—these words are assumed or seen as invisible parts of each statement. This gives the resume a more formal and professional feeling.

- You can create a juicy one-liner to give the reader the most "punch" with the fewest words. For example:

Streamlined manufacturing operations, resulting in a 30% reduction in overhead costs.

- It's okay if your action statements are more than one line long. Two or even three lines long can still be "juicy," but don't go overboard! Put the most interesting and powerful information into your action statements, and save the rest of the story to tell at the **job interview.**

- For example, when the skill is customer relations, the action statement might be:

Developed a more customer-focused approach, providing outstanding service to a diverse clientele, resulting in a significant increase in customer retention, loyalty, and satisfaction.

YES, BUT . . . "I don't know how to write an action statement. What exactly do you mean by an action statement, anyway?"

There are lots of examples in this book, especially in the Sample Resumes section. If you read through them, you'll get a better idea of how to create your own action statements. A strong action statement tells what you did and what results you got from your actions. And of course, this all has to be relevant to your job objective!

Remember those **Key Accomplishment** statements from Step 5? Here's how to transform those accomplishments of the job seeker who wanted to be a Pharmaceutical Sales Rep into more concise action statements.

Before:
- I set a sales record by increasing average monthly sales from $3,000 to $15,000 selling portable exercise equipment, surpassing all of my other team members for any given month in the company's history.
- I built solid relationships with key decision-makers throughout my territory, and expanded the Western territory by 25 percent within my first six months on the job.
- I consulted with physicians, nurses, personal trainers, chiropractors, and massage therapists, using my knowledge of medical terminology to forge strong relationships and make sure they were satisfied with our products.

After:

- Set sales record by increasing average monthly sales from $3,000 to $15,000, surpassing all other team members for any given month in company history.
- Built solid relationships with key decision-makers throughout Western territory, and expanded territory 25% within first six months of hire.
- Consulted with physicians and nurses, using knowledge of medical terminology to forge strong relationships and ensure customer satisfaction.

Here are a few more examples of action statements taken from three different resumes:

- Designed and presented weekly orientation program for career development organization; doubled membership.
- Increased account base by 50% at two locations, through assertive sales leadership and consistent follow-through.
- Established friendly, ongoing relationships with restaurant patrons, building a loyal base of repeat customers.

STEP 7

Arrange your action statements (also known as bullet points) according to the format you chose in Step 3.

If you chose a **chronological format**, place each action statement **under the appropriate job title** where the action or accomplishment took place.

If you chose a **functional format**, place each action statement **under a skill category or heading**. (The Relevant Skills you listed in Step 5 can now become your skill categories.)

If you chose a **hybrid or combination format**, place each action statement under the appropriate job title AND skill heading **within that job title**.

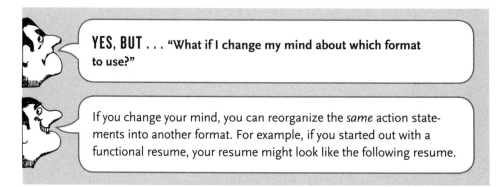

YES, BUT . . . "What if I change my mind about which format to use?"

If you change your mind, you can reorganize the *same* action statements into another format. For example, if you started out with a functional resume, your resume might look like the following resume.

RELEVANT EXPERIENCE

Writing and Editing
- Wrote feature articles for national magazines, including *All About Beer*, as Northern Arizona field editor and photojournalist.
- Edited monthly Letters section for *All About Beer*.

Photography
- Produced product shots and location and personality photos for *All About Beer* magazine.
- Coordinated and directed complex photo shoots.

Then, if you decide that the **chronological resume** would really work better, you could rearrange the action statements in a chronological format, and it might look something like this:

EMPLOYMENT HISTORY

2005–2010   **Writer/Photographer**   *All About Beer* magazine, Phoenix, AZ
- Wrote feature articles on all types of home brewing.
- Edited monthly Letters section.
- Produced product shots and location and personality photos.
- Coordinated and directed complex photo shoots.

Or, if you realize that the **hybrid resume** might be your best bet, you could arrange the action statements like this:

EMPLOYMENT HISTORY

2005–2010   **Writer/Photographer**   *All About Beer* magazine, Phoenix, AZ

Writing and Editing
- Wrote feature articles on all types of home brewing.
- Edited monthly Letters section.

Photography
- Produced product shots and location and personality photos.
- Coordinated and directed complex photo shoots.

Later you can ask for feedback from people working in the field; show them the different formats and ask them which format would work best for you.

These examples illustrate the differences between the three basic resume formats, chronological, functional, and hybrid/combination. You can also refer to the definitions and descriptions in Step 3, pages 6–8.

Whatever format you choose, list your action statements in the order of importance to create a resume that has the most IMPACT on the reader; that is, your first action statement should be the **most impressive or most relevant to your target job.** The next statement should be the next most important, and so on.

List your education, training, and any professional development that is relevant to your target job.

"Education" usually refers to schooling you completed past high school. If you have a degree or completed coursework at a two-year community college, four-year college, or university, list that under Education. "Training" includes apprenticeships, workshops, on-the-job seminars and classes, certificate programs, licenses, correspondence courses, or work-study programs.

"Professional Development" could mean ALL of the above. It's a useful title if you DON'T have a college degree but you HAVE completed coursework, other types of programs, or training related to your target job.

If you are a member of any professional or community organizations that relate to your target job, you can list your memberships under a separate section called "Affiliations" or "Professional Memberships." Or you could list them under "Professional Development," AFTER listing your education and/or training.

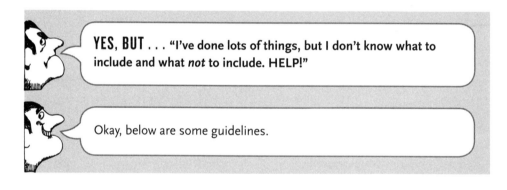

YES, BUT . . . "I've done lots of things, but I don't know what to include and what *not* to include. HELP!"

Okay, below are some guidelines.

Education

- If your education goes beyond high school, include any academic credentials and your degree, even if they aren't directly related to your target job.

- You can mention your college work **even if you haven't graduated or don't plan to get a degree.** Here are some ways to show it:

Accounting Major, Brooks College, Detroit, MI, 2009–2011

University of Phoenix online, B.A. in English, in progress.
Expected graduation: May 2014

Business Coursework: Accounting and Financial Planning
Heald Business College, San Francisco, CA, 2008–2009

Correspondence coursework in the military, equivalent to A.A. in Electronics, 2006

- You should *not* mention your high school unless the target job listing specifically asks for it or you have no other schooling or job-related training to put on your resume.

Training

- If you **completed the training, just list the certification** you earned.

- If you **completed only PART of the training** (or you didn't get a certificate, license, or diploma), **list every course you took** that is **directly related** to your current job objective.

- If you are **new in the field, list every course you took** that is related to your job objective . . . even if you DID complete the training.

- If you have **no job-related training**, and you recently left high school, **list any courses you took in school that show your interest** and commitment to your job goal. You can also list these courses under a "Related Education" heading.

Here are a few more examples of Education, Training, and Memberships:

B.A., Marketing, University of South Florida, Gainesville, FL, 2006

CPR Certification, American Red Cross, 2009

Contractors License #39752, State of Colorado, 2004–present

Additional professional development in Team Leadership, Diversity, and Time Management

Member, Toastmasters International, 2008–present

Board Member, Wilford High School, Wilford, CT, 2003–2008; Board President, 2006–2007

"Education" and "Training" can be listed as separate sections on your resume, or (if they are both short) you can combine them into one section called "Education & Training"! If you have no training, no college experience, and no school courses or other courses that are in any way related to your new job goal, you can leave this section out completely. However, if you do have ANY of the above, you should include it and call this section "Education & Training" or "Professional Development."

>>> **HOT TIP**

When you are listing your education and training, list the degree or name of the certificate or license first, then the name of the school or other place where you received your training and the city and state (if possible). List the year you graduated or received your certification if it's fairly recent (less than ten years ago is a good rule of thumb).

┌─ STEP 9

Summarize your key points at or near the top of the resume.

Now, for the icing on the cake, look over the list you made in Step 2 of the most important qualifications and KSAs (knowledge, skills, and abilities) needed to excel in your target job. Then review your resume for YOUR top skills and strengths. See how the qualifications needed for the job **overlap** with your skills.

Then **write down three or four key points** that **summarize** your experience, skills, and personality traits that will show the new employer **how you are a qualified candidate** for the job.

These points should appear under a heading called "Summary," "Highlights," "Profile," or "Strengths." You could also name this section anything else that is descriptive, such as:

- Summary of Qualifications
- Qualification Highlights
- Career Summary
- Qualifications
- Professional Profile

Put that summary section at the top of your resume, just below your Job Objective, and set each statement off with a bullet.

Here are a couple of examples of Summary sections from other people's resumes:

SUMMARY OF QUALIFICATIONS
- More than seven years of experience in the fashion industry.
- Consistent top producer, with a unique combination of technical expertise and business acumen to achieve excellent sales results.
- Outstanding customer service and relationship-building skills.
- Achieved President's Club status for five consecutive years based on performance.
(Job Objective: Retail Sales Associate, Macy's Women's Department)

QUALIFICATION HIGHLIGHTS
- Award-winning trainer with more than eight years of experience in both corporate and non-profit environments.
- Skilled in assessing training needs, designing comprehensive programs, and delivering dynamic trainings tailored to each business function and organizational level.
- Known for motivational style, team-building skills, and sense of humor.
(Job Objective: Director of Training)

YES, BUT . . . "I don't know what to put in the summary."

A good summary could include:

- Your number of years of experience in the target industry or type of position
- Special education, training, or certification in that target field
- Your key skills, talents, or special knowledge related to the target job
- An accomplishment or recognition that "says it all"
- Something about your personal work style or attitude toward the job that would appeal to an employer

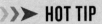

HOT TIP

It's great if you can keep each summary statement to just one or two lines.

HOT TIP

Any time you change your Job Objective (because of a new career opportunity or type of position you are interested in), you will need to review your resume to make sure that the rest of it supports your new objective and keeps your pyramid strong. (See **Appendix D** for help with **customizing your resume** for different opportunities.)

If you think of your resume as a pyramid, your Job Objective is the peak at the top of the pyramid. The Summary section is under the Job Objective and is what the employer generally sees first, so it needs to be a strong support for your Job Objective. Your action statements come next in your Experience section, and they **build the base** of your pyramid, showing the employer what great things you've done that are relevant to your target job.

To be sure you've selected good summary statements, ask yourself:

- Is every item in the Summary section relevant to my job objective?

- Have I supported all of the summary statements through my accomplishment statements in the body of the resume?

In this book's resume samples, you'll find a lot of consistency in the information we have chosen to include in a summary. However, WHATEVER WORKS is a good guideline! You don't have to do it our way if you have a better idea, but the recommendations we've just listed will ensure that you have a strong summary.

Polish and proof—review the whole document and make it shine!

It's a great relief when you feel like your resume is finally done! BUT—before you send it out or show it to anyone, it's got to look PERFECT. That means it has to be clear, accurate, easy to read, and error-free. **It's time to polish and then proofread your resume.**

YES, BUT . . . "I don't know what you mean by 'polishing' my resume. How do I do that?"

As a marketing tool, your resume needs to be visually appealing as well as loaded with accurate, relevant information and accomplishments. A mediocre resume that *looks* good can get more attention than it deserves, while an otherwise excellent resume may be passed over simply for lack of visual appeal. Below are some suggestions for how to make your resume SHINE.

1. Check spelling, grammar, and consistency. One of the top reasons why employers reject job candidates is **finding spelling errors on their resume.** You could be the *ideal candidate* for your *ideal job,* but if your resume is sloppy, with typos and grammatical errors, you could be passed up and lose that great opportunity.

   - Even if you're a great speller, *and especially if you're not,* be sure to check **and double-check** your resume for spelling errors.

   - Review your resume again for grammatical errors. Avoid run-on sentences (sentences that string several sentences together), and watch out for incorrect uses of commas and semicolons.

   - It's fine to use the spell checking tool in your word processing program, but **don't depend on it.** It won't catch a lot of mistakes (such as the classic error "pubic" instead of "public"!), so a second look or a **second pair of eyes** can help. You might ask a friend, a colleague, or another professional to review your resume and look for any errors.

   - Make sure you are consistent in how you list your work history and other elements. This means you must check to make sure that you *always* list the dates the same way (say, 9/08 or September 2008), *always* list your job titles the same way (bold, italics, all capitals, whatever you decide), *always* list the city and state the same way (abbreviated or spelled out), and so on. On a resume, *consistency is king!*

2. Pay attention to how your resume **looks**. If you produce a terrific-looking resume, it will get more attention from an employer (and you'll feel good about yourself every time you look at it!). Playing with the graphic elements of resume writing can be lots of fun. Here are a few Do's and Don'ts to be sure that your resume is easy for an employer to read:

- **Do** choose a font (type style) that is appropriate for the kind of job you're applying for. For example, Times New Roman might be best for a banking job, while Arial is often used in the technology sector.

- **Don't** use more than one font on your resume. Unless you're trained as a graphic designer, too many fonts make a resume visually confusing and unprofessional-looking.

- **Don't** try to cram too much information together. If a resume is too densely packed, it's apt to not get read. Many people think that by cramming lots of information onto one page, they are creating a more impressive resume. But if the employer can't read it, this one goes into the "circular file," no matter how great the content is! Make sure that the text of your resume is big enough for an employer to read. Usually, 11- or 12-point type is fine.

- **Do** use white space generously. Make sure your margins are not too small at the top and bottom, and also on the left and right. Usually, you'll want 1 inch for the left and right margins, and at least .5 inch for the top and bottom margins. You should also insert some white space in between your headings and in between the bullet points. There are different ways to do this, but try to put at least 3 points of white space between the accomplishment statements.

- **Don't** make large sections of text bold or italic; this makes the resume very difficult to read.

- **Do** use bold and italic *judiciously* to emphasize important information.

YES, BUT . . . "I'm afraid my resume will be more than a page long. What should I do?"

Don't worry if your resume goes over one page. First, include all of the information that is impressive and relevant to the new job. *Then* see how much space it takes up. If it goes into page two by only a few lines, then you might want to edit so that it all fits on one page. If your resume is one and a half pages long, that should be fine. If you have lots of related experience, it could be even more powerful to have a two-page resume, to show the depth and breadth of your experience to the future employer.

Here are some ways to think about the ideal length of your resume.

A one-page resume is most appropriate if:

- You are going for a career change to a completely new field in which you have little or no direct experience.

- You are a high school student or a recent grad who has little or no direct work experience in your desired field.

- You are going for a sales position and want to quickly and simply give the reader your top five or so sales accomplishments.

- You are in a field such as law or nursing, in which you do the same thing over and over, so you want to say it just once.

- You know that the prospective employer prefers one-page resumes!

A two-page resume is most appropriate if:

- You are seeking a position that is a step up the ladder in the field in which you already have experience.

- You are going for a mid-level to upper-level position, especially one that requires more than five years of experience.

- You are going for a position that requires multiple skills, including management or supervisory experience; that is, managing others, building or leading a team, and so on.

- Your work experience and accomplishments will not fit easily on one page while keeping your resume visually appealing and easy to read.

- You know that the prospective employer prefers two-page resumes!

Once you have polished your resume, you and a friend, colleague or professional should **review it again** to make sure that it really is finished; that is, accurate, easy to read, and impressive! Then, print out a few hard copies of your new resume. Even though many of us will send our resumes via email or post them online, it's still a good idea to print your new resume on white or off-white paper, using black ink so that it will look good even if it's faxed and/or copied by potential employers. Bring those hard copies with you to your job interviews, so that you have one copy to refer to and a few ready to provide if others show up to interview you!

▶▶► HOT TIP

You'll be able to stay on top of changes in the job search landscape, as well as learn the latest in how to format your resume to send it electronically, by checking out www.damngood.com.

SAMPLE RESUMES

These are actual resumes of real people with whom the authors have worked. Some of the names, dates, and details have been changed to protect the privacy of the job hunter.

(Note: Many more samples can be found at www.damngood.com!)

SAMANTHA B. JENSEN, CNA

1724 East Belleford Street • Brattleboro, VT 08726
(817) 845-1973 • samanthabjensen@gmail.com

Certified Nursing Assistant

SUMMARY OF QUALIFICATIONS

- Compassionate and responsible professional, with both CNA and Acute Care Certification and experience in a clinical setting.

- Particularly skilled in establishing rapport and building excellent relationships with people from diverse ages, cultural and social backgrounds, and levels of need.

- Personable and dedicated, known for outstanding service and attention to detail.

CERTIFICATION & EDUCATION

Certified Nursing Assistant (CNA) Certification
Vermont College of Science & Technology, Brattleboro, VT, 2011

Acute Care Certification
Vermont College of Science & Technology, Brattleboro, VT, 2011

CPR & First Aid Certified, 2010

Coursework toward B.A., American History, Boston College, Boston, MA

Coursework toward B.F.A., Academy of Art College, Northampton, MA

Completed two-year Entrepreneur program, University of Chicago, Chicago, IL

> A recent graduate from a CNA program, Samantha announces her title at the top of her resume, rather than having a Job Objective statement. She also lists her certifications above her work experience, for added emphasis. Samantha's cover **email** is on page 74.

RELEVANT EXPERIENCE

2011   *Full-time Student, CNA Certification Program & Acute Care Certification Program*
Vermont College of Science & Technology, Brattleboro, VT

- Completed all courses and clinical work for two certification programs.

- Provided compassionate and appropriate clinical care to patients from diverse cultural backgrounds and healthcare needs at Edgewood Care Center.

- Clinical care included feeding, bathing, changing bedpans, range of motion exercises, ADLs, use of Hoyer lifts, ambulating, and repositioning the patient.

- Built strong rapport and developed positive relationships with each patient, quickly responding to needs and resolving issues as they arose.

Previous experience includes:

In-home Private Healthcare Provider

- Cared for patient in Springfield, MA, with Duchenne Muscular Dystrophy (DMD), including: Wound care, feeding, administering medicines, personal hygiene, suctioning of trachea, use of Hoyer lifts, respiratory treatments using nebulizer.

- Monitored Alzheimer's patient in Boston, MA, to ensure safety and assisted patient's family with in-home care.

- Provided in-home care to patient in Montpelier, VT, with brain aneurism, including draining and cleaning of colostomy bag and use of catheter.

SOLOMON ARBOURDALE

161 Edinburgh Street
San Francisco, CA 94110

(415) 237-9842
arbourdalesol@earthlink.net
www.arbourdaleart.ccsf.edu/arbour01

CAREER OBJECTIVE   A position in Animation/Multimedia Arts

PROFILE

- A highly creative artist with more than 10 years of experience creating award-winning art using multiple media.
- Organized, able to follow through to complete projects and take initiative to develop new concepts and brainstorm artistic ideas.
- Independent and self-directed, yet also able to collaborate with team members to create exciting comic books and animation.
- Computer skills include: Adobe Photoshop, Illustrator, Flash, and Dreamweaver; Final Cut Pro; Microsoft Word. Adept at quickly learning new skills and technologies.

EXPERIENCE

2001–pres.   **COMIC BOOK ARTIST/WEBSITE DESIGNER,** San Francisco, CA
- Designed interactive, animated website, including all graphics, text, and animation, using Adobe Flash and Dreamweaver.
- Created and published more than 20 comic books, focusing on existential comedy and social/political satire.
- Consistently won top awards each year for all 10 years of the *San Francisco Bay Guardian* Cartoon Contests and for two years of the Marin County Fair Cartoon Contests.
- Invited to create and present art shows of comic books, strips, and animation at numerous Bay Area venues, including:

Cartoon Art Museum	Marin County Fair Building	Balazo Gallery
Artist Television Access	Mission Records	China Books
Art SF	City College of SF Library	

- Cofounded Mission Mini-Comix to coordinate with other artists and publish group works of hard-copy comic books; posted covers on website to reach a wider audience.
- Initiated and led weekly meetings with local comic book artists to brainstorm issues and create copublished work.
- Attended monthly meetings of the Precita Eyes Mural Project, sharing work and ideas with other community artists and organization members.

EDUCATION & TRAINING

Currently enrolled, Multimedia Animation Certification Program
City College of San Francisco, San Francisco, CA
Coursework in Art and Liberal Arts, University of California, Santa Cruz, CA

JOSH BENNETT

177 Doran Drive, #2 • Sacramento, CA 92013

(916) 245-9670 • joshb555@yahoo.com

OBJECTIVE: Wind Technician

SUMMARY OF QUALIFICATIONS

- Highly motivated and energetic professional with a combination of technical, operational, customer service, and leadership skills.

- Articulate communicator, able to establish easy rapport with individuals of all ages, backgrounds, and organizational levels.

- Quick study, with an aptitude for gaining new technical skills. Able to multitask and prioritize effectively to complete projects within tight deadlines.

- Dedicated to participating in new technologies to create a sustainable future. Willing to relocate, and known for working above and beyond the general job responsibilities to further the organizational vision and goals.

RELEVANT EXPERIENCE

Technical & Physical Skills

- Assisted roofers with installation of different types of roofs in all weather conditions, with average roof heights of 50 to 100 feet. (Bennett Roofing)

- Gained a hands-on understanding of structural and technical procedures to ensure safety and proper installation. (Bennett Roofing)

- Worked closely with warehouse staff, using a forklift and other heavy equipment, always maintaining strict adherence to safety guidelines. (Ten Speed Press)

- Regularly lifted and moved 50-pound boxes of books for shipping worldwide. (Ten Speed Press)

- Achieved proficiency in Microsoft Word, Excel, PowerPoint, and Outlook. (United Mortgage Group)

Operations & Administrative Skills

- Evaluated complex rate sheets and performed intricate calculations to determine accurate payments and financial information for clients. (United Mortgage Group)

- Managed the needs and requirements of 200+ high-revenue foreign and domestic accounts. Completed inventory and tracking of goods. Coordinated daily cash flow of $450K or more. (Ten Speed Press)

- Provided administrative support to 5,000 accounts and 80+ Account Executives. Promoted from trainee position within five months. (Wells Fargo)

- Supported sales team, evaluated procedures, and improved processes to streamline operations, resulting in significant improvements in client satisfaction. (Wells Fargo and Ten Speed Press)

-continued-

Operations & Administrative Skills (continued)

- Prioritized workload, created calendar of meetings and events, maintained paperwork, and organized files for clients. (United Mortgage Group)

- Designed and delivered unit and daily lesson plans based on California teaching standards, using a combination of original concepts and existing course materials to foster learning. (Oakland Unified School District)

Leadership & Customer Service Skills

- Applied specialized knowledge to independently respond to inquiries received from clients and other department personnel, including analysis of reports and database research. (Wells Fargo and Ten Speed Press)

- Trained, supervised, and coached a 6-member customer service team. Promoted team members to new positions of challenge and responsibility to foster career development. (Ten Speed Press)

- Directly supervised and trained intern groups of up to 10 each in procedures, programs, and ethics. (United Mortgage Group)

- Built rapport and solid relationships with clients; assessed needs and goals to determine optimal loan packages for each client. (United Mortgage Group)

- Designed and implemented innovative new Resource Department: Matched teachers with specific students and worked with administrators to meet the needs of special education students and their families. (Oakland Unified School District)

WORK HISTORY

2007–pres.   **WELLS FARGO HOME MORTGAGE, Concord, CA**
Client Relations & Administration

2006–07   **UNITED MORTGAGE GROUP, Concord, CA**
Mortgage Broker

2005–06   **OAKLAND UNIFIED SCHOOL DISTRICT/CALVIN SIMMONS MIDDLE SCHOOL, Oakland, CA**
Teacher, Special Education

2000–05   **TEN SPEED PRESS, Berkeley, CA**
Customer Service Manager, Order Department

Previous experience includes:

Roofing Assistant, *Bennett Roofing,* Lanesboro, MA

EDUCATION

B.A., Magna Cum Laude, Child & Adolescent Development
San Francisco State University, San Francisco, CA, 2005

LINDA C. RESPIGHI

1900 East 65th Street, Apt. #12C • New York, NY 10031
(212) 223-5218 • lindacres@comcast.net

OBJECTIVE: A position in Retail Sales

SUMMARY OF QUALIFICATIONS

- More than 10 years of experience and success in sales and marketing, with specific knowledge and expertise in the fashion/beauty industry.

- Skilled in assessing client needs and tailoring sales approach to build excellent relationships and achieve sales goals.

- Highly professional, dependable, and customer-focused, with an emphasis on providing service and ensuring customer satisfaction.

PROFESSIONAL EXPERIENCE

2009–pres.   **CHRISTIAN DIOR BOUTIQUE/BLOOMINGDALE'S,** New York, NY   *Sales Specialist*

- Sold Christian Dior accessories, including handbags, small leather goods, watches, fashion jewelry, and eyewear.

- Built excellent client relationships and a strong repeat and referral client book through attentive service and consistent follow-through.

- Assisted with merchandising and utilized RetailPro and ReLux Expert to manage inventory and complete shift closings.

2008–09   **NORDSTROM,** New York, NY   *Sales Associate*

- Sold full line of St. John designer clothing, including evening, daytime, and sport.

- Increased referral and repeat business by maintaining excellent communication with customers and promoting sales and special events through personal client book.

2005–08   **METRO 200,** New York, NY   *Sales Associate*

- Sold European designer ready-to-wear to a select clientele. Lines include: Cop.Copine, Save the Queen, Isabel De Pedro, and Vassalli.

- Expanded client base and prepared new inventory for sale.

Additional experience includes:

Territory Manager, **JACQUELINE COCHRAN, INC.,** Los Angeles, CA—Sold full fragrance line to department stores, mass volume retailers, and specialty outlets in the Western Region. Brands included L'Air du Temps, Pierre Cardin, and Geoffrey Beene.

Sales Consultant/Macy's Stores, **ESTEE LAUDER, INC.,** San Francisco, CA—Educated customers and sold Estee Lauder treatment products and fragrance line at Macy's Union Square location, providing expert customer service and product knowledge and developing strong client relationships.

Executive Training Program/Assistant Buyer, **SAKS FIFTH AVENUE,** New York, NY—Selected for prestigious internship and promoted to Assistant Buyer based on superior performance.

EDUCATION/PROFESSIONAL DEVELOPMENT

- The Tobe-Coburn School for Fashion Careers, Fashion Merchandising certificate, New York, NY

- A.A., Fine Arts, Averett College for Women, Danville, VA

JILL R. QUINCY

237 Harborside Drive • Baton Rouge, LA 20923
(238) 267-5905 • jrquin23@email.com

OBJECTIVE: Position as Supermarket Cashier or Customer Service Associate

SUMMARY OF QUALIFICATIONS

- More than 10 years of progressive responsibility and experience in the grocery industry.
- Recognized by customers, team members, and management alike for being a knowledgeable and helpful professional. Known for always greeting customers with a smile.
- Dedicated, with a track record of dependability and productivity. Skilled in careful balancing of cash drawers and preparing accurate reports for senior management.

PROFESSIONAL EXPERIENCE

CO-OP SUPERMARKET, Baton Rouge, LA   2002–2012

Retail Clerk

Customer Service

- Developed a reputation for excellent customer service by greeting customers in a friendly and respectful manner, giving them full attention, and taking the time to answer their questions or locating the appropriate personnel to assist them.
- Served as product expert on sophisticated items, directing customers to exotic spices and ingredients, unusual foods, and gourmet items.
- Increased both sales and customer satisfaction in the Natural Foods Department by advising customers on bulk alternatives to name-brand items.

Supervision

- As Head Cashier:
    - Prepared daily schedules for staff of up to 18 cashiers to ensure maximum coverage at checkout locations at all times.
    - Assigned staff to cover peak hours and delegated effectively to provide continuous stocking, ensuring availability of popular items.
- Trained new cashiers in policies, procedures, and customer service techniques.

Administrative

- Balanced four cash drawers daily, with a consistently high level of accuracy.
- As Office Cashier for one year:
    - Balanced books, made deposits, and prepared daily and monthly sales reports.
    - Answered phones and responded to customer and management inquiries.
    - Processed returned checks.

Previous experience includes:

Manager's Assistant, **Wallingford Clothing Store,** Wallingford, CT

> Jill lost her job when her local Co-op Supermarket folded. She felt more confident in her job search after working on this hybrid format resume, which identifies multiple Skill Sets within her experience at Co-op.

EDUCATION

Business coursework, Wallingford Community College, Wallingford, CT

STACEY CARMICHAEL

12 Overton Circle, #5 • Chicago, IL 60615 • (312) 845-4576 • staceycar@aol.com

---

Executive/Personal Assistant

SUMMARY OF QUALIFICATIONS

- More than 15 years providing outstanding administrative and personal support to executives in diverse industries, including financial services, construction, law, and architecture.

- Dedicated, with a strong work ethic; skilled in handling sensitive information with diplomacy and discretion, and maintaining strict confidentiality.

- Organized and resourceful; known for taking initiative, working with minimal supervision, balancing priorities, and accomplishing multiple tasks in deadline-driven environments.

- Computer skills include: Microsoft Office—Word, Excel, PowerPoint, Outlook; Internet Explorer; Lotus Notes; QuickBooks Pro.

PROFESSIONAL EXPERIENCE & ACCOMPLISHMENTS

Executive Assistant Support

- Provided stellar administrative support to financial analyst, hedge fund advisor, and the recognized author of *The LJB Report,* Larry J. Baldwin. Maintained and updated investment portfolio of 200+ files. (LJB)

- Created animated PowerPoint presentations for CEO's public speaking engagements. (LJB)

- Scheduled appointments and maintained calendars. Sorted and distributed mail. (Evansville, LJB, Cloverleaf)

- Tracked projects and investments for boutique investment firm; conducted research; composed correspondence and memos; and greeted executive-level international clients with sensitivity and professionalism. (Cloverleaf)

- Updated and maintained business files; monitored invoicing and followed through with vendors to resolve discrepancies. (Darby, Evansville)

- Drafted and produced legal documents, reports, newsletters, correspondence, customized charts and graphs, invoices, expense reports, and memos for two law partners. Organized law library. (Bristol & Bristol)

- Hired vendors to achieve optimal quality, price, and service; negotiated contracts that resulted in savings of 10–25% per month for each project. (Jones & Sons)

- Prepared complex monthly bank draw and financial reports, including billables and Excel spreadsheets, for 18 multimillion-dollar projects. (Darby)

- Instituted new office procedures and vendor accounts. Ordered supplies and office equipment; set up and maintained filing system. (LJB, Evansville)

- Acted as liaison between office and job site administrative assistant, and assisted bookkeeper in monitoring adherence to budget. (Darby)

- Attended meetings and recorded discussions; transcribed and distributed minutes. (Homeowners Reinsurance)

- Coordinated with caterer, florist, vendors, and entertainment for annual company holiday party. (Darby)

-continued-

Personal Assistant Support

- Coordinated domestic and international travel for business owners and their families; oversaw home maintenance and repairs; maintained personal and social calendars. (LJB, Cloverleaf, Darby)

- Answered multiline phone systems and screened both business and personal calls. (LJB, Cloverleaf, Darby)

- Orchestrated annual 21-member family vacation, coordinating air travel, ground transportation, and accommodations. (LJB)

- Designed and printed 200+ invitations and labels for annual Christmas Tea, and 600+ Christmas cards. Tracked RSVPs and organized social events, including wine selection and seating arrangements. (LJB)

- Updated and maintained Rolodexes of more than 5,000 entries. (LJB)

EMPLOYMENT HISTORY

2009–present *Executive Assistant to Senior Project Manager*
              JONES & SONS CIVIL CONSTRUCTION, Naperville, IL

2007–09   *Executive Personal Assistant/Office Manager*
              DARBY BUILDING COMPANY, INC., Evansville, IN

2006–07   *Onsite Executive Assistant to Owner*
              EVANSVILLE STONEWORKS, INC., Evansville, IN

2003–06   *Executive Personal Assistant to President/CEO*
              LJB CONSULTING, Washington, DC

2002–03   *Legal Administrative Assistant to Partners*
              BRISTOL & BRISTOL, Washington, DC

1998–02   *Executive Assistant to CEO*
              CLOVERLEAF MANAGEMENT, INC., Rockville, MD

Additional experience includes:

Executive Staff Administrator to Vice President, **Homeowners Reinsurance Company,** Rockville, MD

PROFESSIONAL DEVELOPMENT

Graduate, Talbot School of Business, Rockville, MD

Graduate, Katharine Gibbs School, Rockville, MD

Liberal Arts coursework, Rockville Junior College, Rockville, MD

> The functional format enabled Stacey to list her accomplishments in the order of their *relevance* to her job goal, rather than by chronology. She includes the places she worked in parentheses following each action statement, to further strengthen and support her accomplishments. Stacey's cover letter is on page 72.

KEITH L. MARKOWITZ

1701 Applewood Street, #3
Hartford, CT 15432
(203) 577-0430
kmarkowitz@connecticutcollege.edu

OBJECTIVE   Position in Accounting

SUMMARY OF QUALIFICATIONS

- Conscientious and detail-oriented professional with a strong work history and three years of experience in financial services, providing stellar customer service to a diverse clientele.

- Flexible and responsible; skilled in goal-setting, follow-through, and building positive relationships with customers and team members at all organizational levels.

- CPA Exam Eligibility—will complete 150 credit hours and 32 credits of accounting coursework by graduation. Plan to sit for CPA Exam in 2012.

- Relevant computer skills include: Microsoft Excel, Word, PowerPoint, and Outlook.

EDUCATION & CERTIFICATION

B.S., Business Administration - Accounting, Connecticut College, Hartford, CT, 2012

- GPA 3.4

- Coursework includes:

Intermediate Accounting	Advanced Accounting	Audit Accounting
Forensic & Computer Accounting	Tax Accounting	Cost Accounting

- President, Accounting Club, 2011–present

- House Manager, Delta Upsilon Fraternity, 2009–10

Notary Public, State of Connecticut, 2010–present

PROFESSIONAL EXPERIENCE

2008–present **HARTFORD BANK & TRUST,** Hartford, CT   *Teller*

- Traveled to 30+ branches as needed to assist staff with processing transactions and providing an optimal experience for a broad range of bank customers, including corporate, nonprofit, government, and private individuals.

- Assisted team members with branch opening, night deposits, customer deposits, withdrawals, inquiries, ATMs, and issue resolution. Earned additional authority and expanded responsibilities due to integrity and performance.

- Skillfully established rapport and built relationships with long-term customers.

- Consistently exceeded referral goals by assessing customer needs and referring customers to appropriate bank product and service solutions.

- Provided daily support to branch employees to prepare for both internal and external audits, ensuring accuracy of all transactions and positive audit results.

- For special, year-long project, inspected 1,000+ safe deposit boxes and reconciled discrepancies, matching signature cards with documentation to ensure complete, accurate, and up-to-date information as a critical component of audit processing.

CHARLES B. WASHINGTON

964 Ellington Street, #6 • Atlanta, GA 30305
320.750.4302 • cbw27@yahoo.com

OBJECTIVE: Marketing Manager with a focus on Product Development and Branding

PROFILE

- More than 18 years of professional experience in marketing management in the software industry. Expertise includes:

Strategic Business Development   **Creative Branding**   **Global Focus**
Product Design & Development   **Public Relations & Advertising**   **Team Leadership**

- A creative visionary, equally comfortable collaborating in a team environment, working independently, or directing others.

- Analytical problem-solver, able to take initiative to identify and resolve issues and prioritize effectively to complete projects within time and budget.

PROFESSIONAL EXPERIENCE

2004–present   **MANNING MULTIMEDIA, INC.,** London, England
North American Marketing Manager

- Represented Manning Multimedia to U.S. business partners to support their sales and marketing efforts.

- Developed previously unknown astronomy program to the position of market leader.

- Cultivated strategic business relationships, resulting in greater market visibility and expanded business opportunities.

- Presented products to buyers, store manager and consumers at national and international industry trade shows.

- Coordinated advertising and public relations activities and events.

1994–2004   **UNIVERSAL SOFTWARE, INC.,** Atlanta, GA
Marketing Director

- Drove product development strategy: Collaborated with IT on product specifications, and worked with Marketing team to develop innovative branding initiatives.

- Managed sales efforts: Established accounts with distributors and other outlets, including an online program for education site licensing and sales.

- Directed public relations to build awareness and excitement, including press releases, PSAs, reviews, blogs, and both print and online advertising.

- Positioned the company's top product to be the leader in astronomy software.

Previous experience includes:

Special Projects Officer, U.S. Coast Guard, Shreveport, LA
Commander (Retired), U.S. Coast Guard Reserve, Shreveport, LA
Licensed Private Investigator, for Personal Injury Attorneys, Mobile, AL

> A seasoned professional, Charles presents his key areas of expertise at the top of the resume, in the Profile section.

EDUCATION: B.A., Psychology, Georgia State University, Atlanta, GA

A waiter for twenty years, John aims for a major career change, back to his earlier interest in electronics. He'll use this DRAFT resume for some **informational interviewing** (see Appendix B, page 65) to explore ways to gain entry into the field and apply his experience and training from twenty years ago.

JOHN J. DRESHER

2937 Mapleton Alley
Little Rock, AR 33210
(432) 319-8327
johnjd@sbcglobal.net

OBJECTIVE: Position as Electronics Engineering Technician

SUMMARY OF QUALIFICATIONS

- Productive and responsible professional with two years of experience as a radio mechanic, 20 years of expertise in dealing with customers, and a strong commitment to building a career in electronics.
- Quick learner, able to handle multiple tasks and grasp new technologies.
- Skilled in tracing schematic diagrams, analyzing circuits, and troubleshooting.

RELEVANT SKILLS & EXPERIENCE

Electronics Knowledge

- Completed two-year Electronics Engineering Technology program at Herald Technology Institute.
- Taught radio repair to peers in the U.S. Army Signal Corps.
- Rebuilt and rewired electrical home appliances. Replaced a section of house wiring to bring it up to code.
- Completed AutoCAD drafting courses at City College of Little Rock, as well as algebra, geometry, trigonometry, calculus, and physics.

Troubleshooting & Research

- Researched print and online technical manuals and consulted with professionals in the field to resolve technical issues in home and auto repair; used hand tools in woodworking and metalworking as needed to complete all necessary repairs.
- Diagnosed problems in home electronics, including TVs, VCRs, CD and DVD players, and radios.

Customer Relations

- Developed a successful professional approach to providing excellent customer care at Codelle's, consistently applying the following principles:
  - Create an atmosphere that encourages the customer to freely express complaints and concerns.
  - Research potential solutions to each problem, and follow up to ensure customer satisfaction.
- Built positive, ongoing relationships with repeat and referral customers due to outstanding service.

EMPLOYMENT HISTORY

1994–present   **Waiter,** *CODELLE'S RESTAURANT,* Little Rock, AR

1992–1994   **Field Radio Repairman and Instructor,** *U.S. ARMY SIGNAL CORPS,* Houston, TX

EDUCATION & TRAINING

Graduate, Electronics Engineering Technician program, Herald Technology Institute, Little Rock, AR

AutoCAD and drafting coursework, City College of Little Rock, AR

U.S. Army, Field Radio Repair

BRADLEY D. ENGLISH

905.327.3819 • bradenglish2012@comcast.net • www.bradenglishphotography.com

---

JOB OBJECTIVE: Position as Writer/Editorial Assistant/Photographer

KEY STRENGTHS

- More than five years' experience as a published writer, editor, and photographer for multiple media.
- Thorough researcher and effective problem-solver; organized and focused in coordinating and completing projects, consistently ensuring that the job is done right.

RELEVANT PROFESSIONAL EXPERIENCE

Writing & Editing

- Wrote feature articles for national magazines, including *All About Beer,* as the Northern Arizona field editor and photojournalist.
- Wrote Beer Festival Guide for the 14th Annual Phoenix Oktoberfest, published in *Amateur Brewer* and the *Phoenix Sun* and online.
- Created and published a local specialty newsletter for home brewers and collectors, including pub and book reviews, local events and openings, new products, and recipes.
- Selected, copyedited, and proofread manuscripts for Stonehenge Books.

Photography

- Produced product shots and location and personality photos for *All About Beer* magazine.
- Published photo series on Ann Richardson, well-known local author, in *Fiction Monthly* newspaper.
- Photographs selected for *The Elitch Gardens Story,* published by Rocky Mt. Writers Guild, Boulder.
- Contributed photos to the Sierra Club's national slide show, "The Ultimate Environmental Issue."
- Photographed models for the Van Nevsky Talent Agency.

Marketing & Public Relations

- Implemented successful print and online marketing campaigns for Jack London books at Starpower.
- Headed promotion and PR department at Stonehenge Books:
  - Arranged media interviews for new authors; initiated weekly radio program featuring interviews with Stonehenge authors. Orchestrated book-signing publicity events in area bookstores.
  - Wrote press releases and submitted review copies to book columnists.
  - Created mail-order book promotion directed toward special interest groups.

EMPLOYMENT HISTORY

Current: **FREELANCE WRITER/PHOTOGRAPHER,** Phoenix, AZ
Recent assignments for: *Network Marketing; Practical Winery; Amateur Brewer*

2008–2012 **FIELD EDITOR,** *All About Beer* Magazine, Phoenix, AZ

2009–2010 **BOOK SALES REP,** Starpower Press, Tempe, AZ (concurrent with above)

2006–2008 **EDITOR/MARKETING ASSISTANT,** Stonehenge Books, Tempe, AZ

EDUCATION & TRAINING

B.A., Anthropology, Arizona State University, Tempe, AZ

KIIS Broadcasting Workshop, Hollywood, CA

FCC 3rd Class License

> Bradley decided to maintain his privacy by listing only his phone number and email address, but he added his website so that potential employers could see his portfolio online.

MARIA BENJAMIN

2235 Crescent Boulevard • Philadelphia, PA 19103
(215) 321-4275 • mbenjamin@aol.com

OBJECTIVE: Position as Presenter/Trainer for a Health Care organization

HIGHLIGHTS OF QUALIFICATIONS

- Ten years of professional success in health care marketing, and seven years of experience in training design and delivery, including facilitation of an employee training program.
- Warm, down-to-earth teaching style, with a special talent for creating an environment conducive to learning.
- Committed to the educational process, guiding participants to achieve mastery of skills and realization of their own goals.
- Collaborative team member who is also comfortable in leadership roles.

PROFESSIONAL HISTORY & ACCOMPLISHMENTS

2010–pres.   **BLUE SHIELD OF PENNSYLVANIA,** Philadelphia, PA

Health Plan Representative

- Delivered compelling sales presentations to employer groups, outlining Blue Shield benefits package, and contributing to a 2,400+ increase in membership.
- Researched and presented a marketing assessment for Blue Shield Medical Center, well received by joint administrative team and department chiefs.
- Designed and presented seminars for hospital managers on the effective use of management reports to increase department productivity and cost efficiency.

2006–2010   **GREATER PHILADELPHIA HOSPITAL ASSOCIATION,** Philadelphia, PA

Sales Consultant

- Selected as participant trainer at four annual sales conferences to share successful sales strategies with colleagues.
- Delivered dynamic group presentations on productivity tools and metrics at national, regional, and local conferences for health care professionals.
- Earned sales achievement award for three consecutive years.

2005–2006   **HOME CARE OF AMERICA,** Chester, PA

Marketing Director

- Created and conducted quarterly training programs for nonprofessional health care staff, consistent with Medicare standards for home care.
- Presented a marketing overview to senior managers for the Education and Training Department's "Reorientation" program.
- Developed print and online learning materials, including handbooks, exercises, and evaluation forms.

-continued on page two-

2004–2005   **DORADO LABS,** Morristown, NJ

Sales Representative

- Produced largest single sale to new clients from a multihospital system.

- Retained client base without loss for two years—the only representative to accomplish this.

2003–2004   **TEXAS PHARMACEUTICALS,** Dallas, TX

Sales Representative

- Trained nurses, respiratory therapists, and pharmacists on the appropriate use of pharmaceutical products, resulting in increased revenues and a higher quality of patient care.

Previous experience includes:

Supervisor, **Kelly Services**, Dallas, TX

    – Interviewed and tested job applicants.

Dramatics Instructor, **Climb, Inc.**, Chicago, IL

    – Taught creative dramatics, using a lively and engaging approach to foster enjoyment and learning. Trained educators on use of creative dramatics in the classroom.

EDUCATION & PROFESSIONAL DEVELOPMENT

B.A., with honors, **Education/Theater Arts,** University of Chicago, 2000

Time Management Seminar, 2003

Persuasive Selling, 2001, 2002

Negotiation Skills, 2001

> It is easy to see the dates that Maria worked at each job, helping employers to quickly understand her professional history. She received feedback from one employer that her resume was one of the best among forty applicants. Maria's cover letter is on page 73.

ELLIE M. THOMPSON

1402 Grantham Drive • Portland, OR 97520
(503) 762-3847 • elliethompson75@gmail.com

Liturgical Music Director

SUMMARY OF QUALIFICATIONS

- Twenty years of experience and leadership in music and theater production, with more than four years of experience as Music Director in the Catholic Church. In-depth knowledge of Catholic liturgical practice, documents, and hymnody, both traditional and contemporary.

- Skilled in voice, directing adult and children's choirs, keyboard, guitar, and flute, as well as diverse styles of music, including contemporary, gospel, traditional American hymnody, early music, plainchant, and sacred polyphony.

- Known for dynamic leadership and ability to recruit both community and professional participation in music leadership. Able to educate, arrange, and compose music for available talent.

- Dedication to Vatican II principles of full, conscious, and active participation of the assembly. Familiar with Flor y Canto materials and able to lead rehearsals in Spanish; growing experience with Latino musical idioms.

PROFESSIONAL EXPERIENCE

2008–present   **ST. MARY'S CATHOLIC CHURCH,** Portland, OR   *Music Director*

- Plan music and rehearse choirs for weekly and Holy Day Masses in Spanish and English. Accompany choirs on piano, electric organ, and guitar.

- Recruit and train new choir members and instrumentalists. Hire and supervise professional musicians when appropriate.

- Improve performance level of choirs through individual and group vocal coaching.

- Produce choral arrangements and practice CDs as needed.

- Foster a joyful and prayerful experience for both choirs and assembly.

- Provide music for weddings and funerals.

- Collaborate with pastor, liturgy committee, and staff. Work with business manager to establish and track budget for the music program.

- Maintain music library, instruments, and sound system.

- Directed the Schola Cantorum for the Extraordinary Form Mass, both Low and Solemn High Masses, including plainchant Propers.

2005–2008   **SOUTHEAST PORTLAND CHARTER SCHOOL,** Portland, OR   *Music Teacher*

- Taught choir and general music to grades one through eight.

- Wrote music curriculum for the school.

- Produced winter and spring school-wide concerts.

- Directed community choir of parents and teachers.

-continued-

2002–2005   **ST. MARK'S CATHOLIC CHURCH,** Klamath Falls, OR   *Music Director*

- Created and implemented music plans for four weekly Masses, featuring contemporary choir, traditional choir, and cantors. Both choirs performed weekly meditation music after Communion.

- Led weekly rehearsals with choirs and cantors. Expanded cantor ministry; accompanied and trained new cantors.

- Recognized for vibrant and varied programming of contemporary liturgy.

- Coordinated with school choir for Holy Days and selected school liturgies.

- Produced a well-received concert series to raise funds for the purchase of a new piano.

- Maintained music library and all instruments and equipment.

- Developed and tracked music budget, adjusting as needed to ensure alignment with changes in the financial requirements of the church.

Additional professional experience since 1999 includes:

Music Teacher/Choir Director for Catholic and public elementary and middle schools

Alto Soloist and Section Leader

Community Choir Director

Choir Director for other Christian denominations

EDUCATION/PROFESSIONAL DEVELOPMENT

Master's level coursework includes:

Advanced Choral Conducting

Choral Conducting

Choral Literature and Methods

Collegium Musicum: Fifteenth-century sacred polyphony, plainchant, and music of Hildegard von Bingen

B.A., Music, San Francisco State University, San Francisco, CA, 1999

Additional Professional Development includes:

Orff Schulwerk Certification, Level One, Mills College, Oakland, CA, 2000

San Francisco Early Music Society Summer Programs at Dominican College, San Rafael, CA, 1996–2000

Member, Women's Antique Vocal Ensemble (WAVE), Berkeley, CA

Member, Illumina chant performance group, Albany, CA

Produced two concerts for the Feast of the Assumption: In Her Praise, Portland, OR, 2006, and Ave Maris Stella, Portland, OR, 2005

ROBERT VELASQUEZ

536 Sylvan Avenue • Los Angeles, CA
(310) 254-7632 • robvelasquez@gmail.com

OBJECTIVE

Position as Park Supervisor with Regional Park District

CAREER SUMMARY

- Over 25 years of professional experience in horticulture, with in-depth knowledge of landscaping and plants. Lifelong interest and background in gardening.

- A dedicated and conscientious supervisor, skilled in training team members and fostering excellence.

- Organized, with a proven record of reliability in coordinating and completing multiple projects to achieve overall objectives.

- Skilled negotiator and public speaker, able to build positive relationships with community groups, schools, and individuals from diverse cultural and organizational backgrounds.

RELEVANT EXPERIENCE

Supervision, Training, & Safety

- As Landscape Maintenance Supervisor at Copeland Landscaping:
  - Supervised and scheduled 35 permanent gardeners and 11 foremen.
  - Trained and evaluated employees, teaching safe use of power tools, principles of horticulture, and chemical pest control.

- Supervised 20–40 gardeners at Brookwood Hospital, including both youth and adults:
  - Presented safety guidelines at mandatory weekly safety meetings.
  - Monitored attendance and productivity.
  - Taught pruning techniques, weed control, and turf management.
  - Orchestrated field trips to local botanical sites.

- Trained and coached hundreds of seasonal gardening helpers, including U.C.L.A. students working at the Botanical Gardens.

Technical Experience

- Operated gas and electric equipment and power tools throughout career, including mowers, edgers, generators, tractors, chain saws, weed eaters, brush cutters, turf equipment, and trimmers.

- Maintained grounds and greenhouses at U.C.L.A. Botanical Gardens, including construction, repair, plumbing, irrigation, tree removal, erosion control, fertilization, rototilling, pest and weed control, mowing, sprinkler system installation, pruning, and maintenance of athletic fields.

- Repaired Los Angeles Unified School District truck and maintained an excellent driving record.

- Maintained indoor plants at Copeland Landscaping and at school administration offices.

-continued on page two-

Community Relations

- Led informative tours of the Botanical Gardens for student groups and garden clubs, incorporating a sense of wonder to inspire participants.

- Acted as liaison among gardeners, district teachers, and administrators, as union shop steward at Los Angeles Unified School District.

- Mediated minor grievances and approved landscaping requests of homeowners' association, as Landscape Maintenance Supervisor for Copeland Landscaping.

Administration

- At Copeland Landscaping:

  - Submitted daily reports covering inspection of work sites, damage, equipment usage, and materials needed.

  - Interviewed and hired gardeners; verified and submitted weekly time sheets to ensure accurate and on-time payment.

- For Los Angeles Unified School District:

  - Selected botanical sites and coordinated field trips for students.

  - Organized appreciation dinners for retiring gardeners.

  - Served on negotiating team for union contracts.

EMPLOYMENT HISTORY

1999–2011	*Gardener/Assistant Foreman* *Gardener Caretaker (live-in)*	**Los Angeles Unified School District,** **Kingman Science Center,** Los Angeles, CA
1996–1999	*Landscape Maintenance Supervisor*	**Copeland Landscaping, Inc.,** Hollywood, CA
1995–1996	*Head Gardener*	**Brookwood Hospital,** Laguna Beach, CA
1985–1995	*Nurseryman*	**Botanical Gardens, U.C.L.A.,** Los Angeles, CA

EDUCATION & TRAINING

Horticultural coursework, Los Angeles Community College: Horticulture, Greenhouse Management, Plant Diseases, and Herbicide-Resistant Plants

Horticulture workshops through U.C.L.A. Botanical Gardens: Plant Identification, Plant Maintenance, Propagating, and Spraying

Supervisory Training, Los Angeles Unified School District

CPR and First Aid Certified

Beverly's new resume and cover letter were key components of her *reentry* into the type of position she had held prior to becoming a full-time parent. Beverly's cover letter appears on page 70.

BEVERLY R. HAMILTON

4347 East 61st Street • Cincinnati, OH 57530
(213) 348-9342 • brhamilton4347@yahoo.com

OBJECTIVE: Administrative Assistant, Law Firm

SUMMARY OF QUALIFICATIONS

- More than 10 years of experience providing outstanding administrative support in diverse environments, including two years as a recruiting coordinator for a Cincinnati law firm.
- Highly motivated, organized, and detail-oriented, equally comfortable with team collaboration and working independently. Known for excellent prioritizing and multitasking to achieve on-time completion of tasks and projects. Computer literate in Microsoft Word and Internet applications.
- Personable and professional, skilled in effectively representing the organization, establishing rapport with clients and colleagues, and maintaining confidentiality.

RELEVANT SKILLS & EXPERIENCE

2009–present **NORDSTROM,** Cincinnati, OH   *Sales Associate*

- Greeted both existing and prospective clients, established rapport, and sold designer women's apparel to a high-end local and national clientele.
- Answered phones and fielded inquiries; attended runway shows and product knowledge meetings. Replenished stock and tidied rooms after client use.
- Wrote and distributed letters and emails to clients, including announcements of upcoming events, thank-you notes, and personalized invitations.

1999–09   **BOARD & EXECUTIVE COMMITTEE APPOINTMENTS/FULL-TIME PARENT**
Bel Canto High School, Cincinnati, OH   2006–09
- Chair, Matadors Club: Tracked gifts from major donors and wrote thank-you letters.

The College Preparatory School, Cincinnati, OH   2002–06
- Elected President and Vice-President of Parents Association:
  - Wrote meeting agendas and facilitated Executive and regular Board meetings.
  - Coordinated event calendar, delivered speeches and presentations at school events, and wrote monthly column in the school newspaper, *The Periscope*.

Sinclair Elementary School, Cincinnati, OH   1999–02
- Provided classroom and administrative assistance to teachers and school administrators.

Previous professional experience includes:

RECRUITING COORDINATOR, *Stein, Falcon & Morgan, Attorneys at Law,* Cincinnati, OH
Collaborated with partner to administer Fall On-Campus Recruiting and Summer Internship programs:
- Coordinated attorney travel and scheduling for on-campus interviews throughout the United States.
- Processed and evaluated student resumes. Contacted students and scheduled in-house appointments; coordinated travel for visiting candidates. Prepared offer and rejection letters as needed.
- Acted as primary administrative contact for new interns and conducted orientations to acclimate interns to the office environment, policies, and procedures.
- Prepared and presented expense tracking and reports, ensuring adherence to budgetary requirements.

EDUCATION: B.A., History, University of California, Berkeley, CA

CAROL ANN DONOVAN

24573 South Fork Road
Ann Arbor, MI 50370
(431) 276-0889
cadonovan@aol.com

OBJECTIVE: Position as Apprentice Baker

STRENGTHS

- A creative professional with a passion for food, committed to producing the highest-quality products.
- Flair for design and presentation. Experienced in retail sales and merchandise display.
- Hard-working and dedicated, able to learn new skills quickly and take on additional responsibilities.
- A team player with a strong work ethic, a positive attitude, and a sense of humor.

EXPERIENCE

Cooking Knowledge

- Studied with Master Chef Ken Wolfe and learned:
  - Principles, techniques, and timing of food preparation
  - The importance of quality and freshness of ingredients
  - Chemistry and the effects of combining ingredients
  - Balancing flavors within a dish and within a meal
  - Innovative approaches to traditional cooking principles

> Because Carol Ann has no paid experience as a baker, she uses the functional format to highlight her cooking knowledge and other relevant skills. And because she has no degree or special certification, she lists her relevant coursework under the heading of Professional Development.

Coordination & Teamwork

- Supervised and maintained a balanced flow of inventory for the Renaissance Theater Group and The Gift Box.
- Monitored sales and ordered supplies to ensure correct stocking and display. Performed telephone and online research to determine best prices for each item.
- As Store Manager, coordinated timing and priority of tasks, and worked closely with a finely tuned sales team to provide an outstanding customer experience.

Speed & Accuracy

- Prepared puff pastry dough in cooking class, consistently completing in record time.
- Sold a high volume of theater tickets and retail merchandise in minimal time.
- Accurately counted, recorded, and deposited cash receipts for retail store.

WORK HISTORY

2007–pres.	*Store Manager/Assistant Manager*	THE GIFT BOX, Ann Arbor, MI
2003–2006	*Theater Manager/Sales Associate*	RENAISSANCE THEATER GROUP, Ann Arbor, MI

PROFESSIONAL DEVELOPMENT

Liberal Arts coursework, Langley Community College, Langley, MI, 2001–2003

Classes in Cooking Principles with Master Chef Ken Wolfe, 2009

TANDRA SINGH

1172 E. Jackson Street • Miami, FL 33222
(825) 347-3754 • tandrasingh@gmail.com

OBJECTIVE: A position in Development/Fundraising

SUMMARY OF QUALIFICATIONS

- Florida native with more than eight years of experience in both corporate and nonprofit environments, and a track record of success as Assistant Producer, On-Air Fundraising and Assistant Development Director at WQZQ Radio.

- Creative, organized, and client-focused, with excellent research, telephone, and personal communication skills. Able to quickly connect with individuals from diverse cultural, organizational, and socioeconomic backgrounds.

- Skilled team leader, able to train and guide team members using a straightforward approach and a sense of humor to achieve top performance and create a vibrant, cohesive work environment.

PROFESSIONAL HISTORY & ACCOMPLISHMENTS

WQZQ RADIO, Miami, FL   2003–present
Assistant Development Director/Assistant Producer/Underwriter/Volunteer Coordinator

- Promoted from volunteer for pledge drives to Underwriter, Assistant Producer, and Assistant Development Director.

- Cultivated relationships, secured media sponsorships, and negotiated underwriting spots with local, national, and international arts organizations, including the United Nations Film Festival, Miami Symphony, Comedy Improv, and Center for the Book.

- Solicited donations from vendors and sponsors for the semiannual pledge drives, generating $250K to $325K during each drive.

- Trained volunteers for special events and fostered a lively, fun, and productive work environment.

- Conducted cold-calling and negotiated with vendors to advertise their products, services, and events on WQZQ.

- Achieved special recognition from the General Manager for securing the most advertising revenue in the station's history.

- Responded to listener questions and concerns, providing information and referrals to appropriate personnel and resources as needed to support a positive listener experience.

- Researched and recommended news stories for weekly broadcasts.

Previous experience includes:

Reservations/Front Desk/Revenue Accountant, **ALHAMBRA HOTEL,** Miami, FL

Front Desk/Concierge, **EL SOMBRERO HOTEL,** Miami, FL

News Monitor/Video Editor, **AUDIO VIDEO REPORTING (AVR),** Gainesville, FL

EDUCATION & PROFESSIONAL DEVELOPMENT

B.A., Political Science, Florida State University, Hollywood, FL

Master's Certificate in Online Marketing, University of Florida, Gainesville, FL

International Studies Program, American University, Copenhagen, Denmark

Certificate in Hotel Management, Shoreline Community College, Hollywood, FL

June Lynch

2600 Ptarmigan Drive, #3 • Walnut Creek, CA 94595 • (925) 835-8991 • juntim@aol.com

OBJECTIVE

Counseling Position with a focus on older adults, including:

Grief & Loss　　　Aging & Life Transitions　　　Health & Wellness　　　Self-Esteem

SUMMARY OF QUALIFICATIONS

- Nine years of counseling experience with adults and couples, with an emphasis on grief and loss.
- Highly motivated, resourceful, and enthusiastic. Skilled in building relationships with clients of all ages and cultural backgrounds.
- "She is a person who emanates compassion, warmth, down-to-earth presence, sense of humor, and dedication to her work." —Eike Diebold, Ph.D., Redwood Center, Berkeley, CA

EDUCATION

M.A., Psychology, California State University East Bay, Hayward, CA

B.A., magna cum laude, Psychology, Holy Names College, Oakland, CA

Certified Grief Counselor, American Academy of Grief Counseling, Niles, OH

June uses the functional format in a different way, selecting a few places she has worked as subheadings to organize and highlight her accomplishments. Now in her eighties, she has used this resume many times to secure the unique PART-TIME employment she seeks.

RELEVANT EXPERIENCE

Namaste/Shanti Project:

- Counseled individuals experiencing deep grief and loss, providing a safe space and compassionate listening.
- Co-led trainings for volunteers to emotionally and psychologically prepare them for working with grieving clients. Used role-playing, practice sessions, and shared personal experience of loss. Educated volunteers in the vocabulary of grief, and fostered a supportive environment.

Holy Redeemer Center:

- Provided short-term and long-term counseling for adults moving through life transitions, including grief, relationship, and esteem-building issues.
- Co-authored master business plan and acted as Development Director. Wrote winning grants that substantially strengthened the financial viability of the retreat center.
- Received recognition from supervisor, colleagues, and clients: "A particular affinity for working in a focused, problem-solving style. Her down-to-earth and direct manner, warmth, and sense of humor, as well as her wealth of life experience, are all assets in her work." —Supervisor Deborah B. Ghidinelli, M.S.

Redwood Center:

- Assessed client needs and created proactive plans for individuals and couples to achieve greater satisfaction in their work and personal relationships.

WORK HISTORY

2007–pres.	**ST. MARY'S CENTER,** Oakland, CA	*Support Group Co-leader*
2005–07	**BAY AREA PSYCHOLOGICAL SERVICES (BAPS),** Berkeley, CA	*Counselor*
2001–05	**REDWOOD CENTER,** Berkeley, CA	*Counselor*
1998–01	**HOLY REDEEMER CENTER,** Oakland, CA	*Counselor/Dev't. Director*

Previous experience: Four years as *Grief Counselor* with **Namaste, a division of Shanti Project,** Oakland, CA

David found the hybrid format
to be a powerful way to quickly
convey his skills and achievements
over his extensive career at UPS.
David's cover email is on page 74.

DAVID B. CHENG

4240 San Filipo Drive
St. Louis, MO 60036
314.387.2147
chengdavidb@gmail.com

OBJECTIVE

Leadership position in Information Technology, with a focus on:

Operations & Process Improvement   **Customer Satisfaction**   **Team Leadership**

SUMMARY OF QUALIFICATIONS

- Highly motivated, organized, and effective IT professional with more than 17 years of progressive experience in developing and implementing IT solutions to meet changing needs and priorities at all organizational levels.
- Analytical problem-solver, able to quickly identify and troubleshoot technical challenges and maintain complex hardware and software systems.
- Skilled in building productive, cohesive teams, leading by example and providing guidance and mentorship to improve individual and team performance and career development.
- Articulate, energetic communicator and presenter, able to design effective presentations to meet the needs of diverse technical and business audiences. Skilled in translating across functions to maximize understanding and buy-in.

PROFESSIONAL EXPERIENCE

UNITED PARCEL SERVICE (UPS), St. Louis, MO & Kansas City, MO   **1995–present**

Industrial Engineering Manager	*2006–present*
Information Technology Manager	*2004–06*
Information Technology Specialist/Account Executive, Solutions Group	*2002–04*
Technician I & II/Lead Technician	*1999–02*
Trainer	*1995–98*

Consistently promoted to greater levels of responsibility and leadership based on outstanding performance, analytical skills, and team-building capabilities.

Operations & Process Improvement

- Collaborated with district managers to consolidate four Help Desk centers into one regional center, achieving smooth transition without service interruption.
- Championed initiative to increase Customer Service Index score and meet district Plan of Action goals. Achieved immediate success and gained recognition from Department Head for significant and rapid improvement.
- Improved Service Level Agreements on service orders from 92% to 98%, achieving a considerable increase in timely problem resolution for all customers.
- Reviewed, modified, and enhanced all organizational and technical policies and procedures as well as technical systems and implementation processes.

-continued-

Operations & Process Improvement (continued)

- Brainstormed with management team to initiate and implement process improvements that increased productivity and reduced costs.
- Worked closely with Operations Manager to develop, implement, and monitor detailed Operating Plans to optimize work flow and production. Adjusted plans based on feedback and performance, and rolled out plan district-wide.
- Reduced Cost to Serve support for PCs from $119 to $70 per PC by eliminating underused equipment, reducing overtime through "staggered start" scheduling, improving cost controls, and instituting better monitoring of existing equipment.
- As member of Solutions Group, presented IT solutions to managers of Operations, Sales, Brokerages, International Operations, Accounting, and Auditing, and responded to questions regarding the integration of the existing ERP system.

Training, Coaching & Team Building

- As IT Manager, organized and led a staff of 30 Computer Technicians responsible for all Missouri operations.
- As Lead Technician, directed a productive and closely integrated staff of four supporting 1,500 employees in multiple operational functions and work environments.
- Developed and implemented effective orientations for new hires, and created technical training programs for existing staff on optimal utilization of equipment, resulting in increased efficiency, team development, and knowledge sharing.
- Resolved staffing and attendance problems by negotiating and coordinating alliance with outside company, prioritizing effectively, and instituting employee incentives, resulting in excellent performance and on-time completion of all work.
- Designed and delivered dynamic, informative presentations to introduce new technologies to diverse audiences, tailoring presentation style to meet the needs of each group, from line staff through senior executive levels.
- Led team effort to improve IT Department's rank from 54 out of 55 into the Top 10 corporate ranking.
- Increased IT Assessment score from 58% effective to 78% effective, and increased Hub Assessment score from 68% effective to 81% effective.
- Improved Employee Relations Index score from 56% favorable to 82% favorable.
- Consistently sought out by peers for technical and troubleshooting support, and general problem-solving.

PROFESSIONAL DEVELOPMENT

MCSE Preparation Course at University of Missouri, Kansas City, MO

Business Coursework at University of Missouri, Kansas City, and Chabot College, St. Louis, MO

Training in computer technology, data management, and quality tracking and analysis software

Computer skills: Microsoft Office Suite, UPS proprietary software applications, A+ Certified

TOMAS L. HERNANDEZ

67 Oak Tree Circle, #347 • San Antonio, TX 73686
(525) 238-3761 • tomas.hernandez376@hotmail.com

OBJECTIVE: Position as Sales/Account Manager

PROFILE

- More than 10 years of success as a strategic sales leader, business driver, and account manager in multiple industries across both domestic and global markets.
- Confident new business developer with expertise in establishing and nurturing relationships of trust with C-level decision-makers.
- Communicate effectively at all levels; able to assess customer business drivers, translate technical knowledge into business terminology, and position products to deliver the best value proposition and maximize ROI.
- Core competencies include:

Strategic Account Management	Client Relationship Management
Consultative Sales	Solutions Selling
Customer Engagement	New Business Development
Strategic Pricing	Contract Negotiations

PROFESSIONAL EXPERIENCE & ACHIEVEMENTS

SAN ANTONIO SOFTWARE, INC., San Antonio, TX   2009–present

Account Manager

Challenged to reignite account sales across North America.

- Developed business strategies and leveraged extensive network of contacts to feed the sales pipeline, generate and qualify sales leads, and win new business.
- Partnered with Subject Matter Experts to market complex enterprise software solutions and drive significant sales improvements.
- Championed the largest new logo license deal for FY 09, valued at $1.1M:
  - Proposed an enterprise initiative to replace San Antonio Energy's current product and positioned San Antonio Software on their bid list.
- Retained a key customer that had considered terminating their contract when they reached their capacity limit:
  - Forged a strategy to increase the number of licenses from 1,000 to 2,500.
  - Negotiated a contract for a single license fee of $956K with no additional expenses.

SUSTAINABLE ENERGY SOLUTIONS, Austin, TX   2008–2009

Senior Sales Executive

Recruited to drive sales in the solar, wind, and natural gas vertical markets, applying the "best of breed" approach to identify and present successful enterprise solutions to top decision-makers.

- Increased the sales pipeline from $0 to $2.5M by strategically identifying new opportunities within the territory.
- Generated $400K in new revenue, on target for 100% of quota, primarily due to expert account management, contract renewal, and additional licensing.
- Initiated talks with western partners regarding an enterprise-wide system upgrade, and proposed pipeline management services to key client. Supervised all license sales and professional services across the U.S. to assigned account list.

-continued-

R&R ENTERPRISE SOFTWARE, INC., Dallas, TX   2004–2008

Account Manager, DSM Products

Joined the organization to revitalize select territories in Canada and recapture key enterprise accounts, targeting telecom, banking, and Canadian federal government. Cultivated executive contacts and negotiated with procurement specialists in the public, private, and federal sectors.

- Repeatedly delivered 100% of quota or above, achieving $600K for the partial year of 2005, $3.25M in 2006, and $3.68M in 2007.
- Retained a major customer and sold a $5.6M solution:
  - Demonstrated to technical team and key decision-makers how to maximize mainframe and distributed systems capacity.
  - Won the "Getting It Done" Director's Award and Q4 Field Leadership Bonus.
- Structured two sales with major client in financial services sector: Upgraded a partner's software solution and provided a network monitoring tool, for $1M in total revenue.
- Recaptured Canada Revenue Agency from a competitor and closed a $500K sale. Renegotiated licensing to provide more product and higher capacity for the same spend, resulting in excellent customer satisfaction.
- Negotiated a multiyear maintenance agreement with the federal Defense Security Service, to provide additional product and capacity worth $750K annually.
- Monitored and maintained strict compliance with revenue recognition and vendor-specific objective evidence (VSOE).

Previous experience includes:

Sales Administrator, **Standard Switchgear Company,** Dallas, TX

  - Engineered and standardized a $3M medium-voltage soft start switchgear package for a firm building natural gas compressor skids. Captured $900K in incremental revenue by providing expertise to customers during the design build process of an OEM application.

Sales Specialist, **Southwestern Distribution, Inc.,** Dallas, TX

  - Generated more than $1M in new incremental revenue by initiating and closing sales of LV motor control centers to municipalities and wastewater treatment plants.
  - Provided leadership as the "Switchgear Guru," and structured sales of commercial switchgears and lighting projects to school districts, securing $500K in new revenue.

Outside Sales Representative, **Herald Electric,** Dallas, TX

  - Exceeded revenue goal of $2.6M and increased spend from one customer by 36% to $600K over prior year through strategic positioning and expert relationship management.

EDUCATION & PROFESSIONAL DEVELOPMENT

B.S., Industrial Distribution, Texas A&M University, College Station, TX

Information Technology Infrastructure Library (ITIL) Certified

Additional professional development includes:

Real World Selling, by Rick Allan & Associates

Sandler Sales Training, by Sandler Systems, Inc.

Because he is looking for a position in the Education field, Ruben puts his own education at the top of his resume. Ruben's cover letter is on page 71.

RUBEN A. SARAGOSSA

7241 Selma Street, #325
Minneapolis, MN 59708
(902) 358-7967
rubensaragossa14@globalemail.net

OBJECTIVE: Position as High School Principal

EDUCATION

M.A., School Administration, University of Minnesota, Minneapolis, MN
B.A., History & Physical Education, University of Minnesota, Minneapolis, MN

Lifetime Teaching Credentials: General Elementary and Secondary
Lifetime Administrative Credentials: Standard, Elementary, and Secondary

CAREER SUMMARY

- Eighteen-year background in administration at the State Department of Education and at high school and university levels, including three years as the Principal at a large, very diverse high school.

- Experienced in strategic direction, curriculum development, academic leadership, daily operations, personnel evaluation, and partnering with parents, local organizations, and community groups.

- A creative and "take charge" administrator, skilled in identifying issues and initiating programs that yield outstanding results for students, teachers, the school, and the community.

PROFESSIONAL EXPERIENCE & ACCOMPLISHMENTS

2008–present   **ASSISTANT PRINCIPAL, Harrison High School,** Minneapolis, MN

- Conceived and implemented a successful plan for dropout prevention, featuring individualized instruction for truant and high-risk students. Results:

  – Elimination of disruptive classroom behavior

  – Reduction in after-school detention

  – Improvement of the educational atmosphere

  – Increased revenues for ADA

- Recovered over $200,000 in ADA revenues for the school district: Restructured work schedule of the attendance technician to provide time and facilities for documenting legitimate absences.

2006–2008   **MANAGEMENT INTERN, AMFAC Corporation,** Food Division, St. Paul, MN

- Trained staff and developed personnel for middle management positions.

2004–2006   **DIRECTOR, SPECIAL PROJECTS, Central School District,** St. Paul, MN

- Oversaw implementation and evaluation of federal and state special projects and programs for the district, including programs for underserved and at-risk elementary and secondary students.

Continued on page two

RUBEN A. SARAGOSSA

Page two

2001–2004   **PRINCIPAL, North School,** St. Paul, MN

- Initiated the updating of course descriptions and expansion of course offerings to accommodate the needs of both low achievers and gifted students.

- Originated and coordinated a highly successful "Career Day" program, which exposed students to a broad range of occupations and helped teachers link relevant subject matter to the world of work.

- Spearheaded a fundraising drive to replace antiquated equipment for the school football field: Coordinated the joint efforts of parents, students, community business leaders, and city officials; raised $30,000.

- Increased ADA revenues by $45,000 by initiating an in-school study hall program, which tremendously reduced class-cutting and improved overall student grades.

- Significantly reduced youth gang activity on campus by bringing together a task force of parents and community representatives, including state legislators and local law enforcement agencies.

- Initiated the formation of a minority student club to increase participation in campus activities. Results:

  - Increased self-esteem of minority students

  - Election of the first Hispanic female student body president

  - Development of a stabilizing force for working with youth gangs

  - Involvement of minority students in sponsorship of a popular annual talent show

- Won recognition for providing outstanding and effective leadership.

1999–2001   **ASSISTANT PRINCIPAL, CURRICULUM, South High School,** Minneapolis, MN

- Developed and coordinated Master Schedule.

- Chaired the District's Student Attendance Review Board.

- Represented South High on the District Professional Curriculum Committee.

1995–1999   **EDUCATIONAL CONSULTANT, State Department of Education,** Minneapolis, MN

- Led instructional team in the design and review of curriculum for educationally disadvantaged students throughout Minnesota.

- Oversaw disbursement of $18.3 million for statewide compensatory education programs.

1992–1995   **PROJECT DIRECTOR, University of Minnesota,** Minneapolis, MN

- Coordinated and developed a pilot program funded by the federal government to create a GED curriculum for high school dropouts; successfully recruited and placed students in college, job training programs, and jobs.

PROFESSIONAL AFFILIATIONS

Association of Minnesota School Administrators

United Administrators of Minneapolis/St. Paul

Christina Lauderberg

9902 Deschutes Avenue, #7A • Des Moines, IA 59536
(406) 438-2507 • cmlauderberg27@gmail.com

OBJECTIVE

Position as German language instructor, with a focus on:
Classroom Teaching, Academic Counseling, Curriculum Development, and Course Evaluation

QUALIFICATIONS

- Five years' experience teaching German at all levels to diverse individuals and groups, customizing approach for different learning styles.
- Strong practical and theoretical knowledge; confident in development and selection of innovative teaching materials to facilitate learning.
- Dynamic classroom presentation and team teaching approach, with proven effectiveness in program design and administration.
- Certified trainer for student teachers.

RELEVANT ACCOMPLISHMENTS

Teacher/Language Instructor   2007–present
Hamburg Volkshochschule, German as a Second Language Department, Hamburg, Germany

CLASSROOM TEACHING

- Taught German as a Second Language to Beginning, Intermediate, and Advanced students in varied settings, including: Male offenders in a correctional facility, female Spanish-speaking residents of Germany, and foreign laborers in employment advancement courses.
- Employed a vibrant teaching style to engage students and facilitate learning, and tailored approach to address the learning style and needs of each student.

COUNSELING & TRAINING

- Trained student teachers in effective classroom techniques, and led seminars on didactic issues.
- Advised adult immigrant students on complex personal and academic issues, including immigration and employment regulations, housing and landlord concerns, entrance exams and class level placement, and health and medical resources.

CURRICULUM DEVELOPMENT & COURSE EVALUATION

- Evaluated course and improved existing German as a Second Language curriculum, incorporating more diversity to respond to students' needs and interests.
- Conducted academic research focusing on rules of grammar and on speaking, reading, writing, and listening comprehension.

Substitute Nurse, *Anscharhohe Eppendorf Nursing Home,* Hamburg, Germany   2004–2007

EDUCATION & CREDENTIALS

Equivalent of Master's Degree in German Language, University of Hamburg, Hamburg, Germany
Credentials to teach students through tenth grade
Relevant coursework: German, Pedagogy, Politics

A. J. KAROLA

45 Seventh Street, #3B • Berkeley, CA 94701
(510) 462-1688 • ajkarola@mind.net

OBJECTIVE: A position as a Line Cook

SUMMARY OF QUALIFICATIONS

- An experienced line cook, known for dedication and commitment to quality in food preparation and presentation.

- An organized team player, able to take initiative to support team members and complete multiple tasks within tight deadlines.

- Eager to learn new skills and able to adapt to different environments.

- Creative and passionate about food and cooking.

PROFESSIONAL EXPERIENCE

2009–11 **BEACH CHALET RESTAURANT & BREWERY,** San Francisco, CA
Line Cook

- Prepared fresh, high-quality food for a diverse clientele at this fast-paced, high-volume restaurant, serving 1,000+ patrons on weekends.

- Stocked and monitored ingredients to ensure quality and quantity, communicating with sous chefs and other line cooks to maintain appropriate inventory levels.

- Took initiative to work at all stations and gain additional experience, including pantry, sauté, grill, and fry.

- Awarded raise based on excellent performance, commitment to quality, and care in food preparation.

2008 **VALENTINA'S RISTORANTE,** Berkeley, CA
Line Cook/Prep Cook

- Prepared traditional Northern Italian recipes and handmade pizzas at this intimate neighborhood restaurant with a loyal repeat customer base.

- Provided a strong focus on quality, freshness, and presentation of each order.

2006–08 **SUNSET RESTAURANT CHER-AE HEIGHTS CASINO,** Trinidad, CA
Line Cook/Prep Cook

- Worked grill, fry, and pantry stations and prepared soups, salads, and desserts, featuring seasonal California cuisine.

2004–05 **BRIO BREADWORKS,** Arcata, CA
Shaper/Baking Assistant

- Shaped dough, prepared additional ingredients, and baked loaves of bread, assisting baker as needed and preparing finished loaves for delivery.

EDUCATION: B.A., Liberal Arts, Humboldt State University, Arcata, CA, 2008

DOUGLAS MATSUSHITA

2903 Hawthorne Street
Raleigh, NC 32730
(305) 296-0897
dougmatsu@gmail.com

Doug used Arial for his resume, a very popular font in the technology sector. He listed his knowledge of computer systems, programs, and languages on page one under the heading of Technical Profile.

Senior Software Engineer

SUMMARY OF QUALIFICATIONS

- More than 12 years of experience writing clean, flexible, and reusable code to create powerful applications and tools for consumers and internal use.

- Creative, analytical, and detail-oriented; able to identify needs and develop solutions that meet programming and project requirements.

- Excellent communicator and team member, skilled in collaborating to achieve objectives and explaining complex technical concepts to nontechnical users.

- Motivated and self-directed; adept at quickly learning new technologies and completing multilayered projects within tight deadlines.

TECHNICAL PROFILE

Proficient in: Windows API, .NET, COM, COM+, ATL, MFC, SIP, RTP, VoIP, MRCP, TCP/UDP sockets, Dialogic API, XML, ODBC, DirectX, RenderWare Graphics

Languages: C/C++, C#, Python, SQL, Scheme

Programs: Microsoft Visual C++, Visual SourceSafe, and Project; Metrowerks CodeWarrior, WinDbg, Subversion, CVS, Alienbrain, SWIG, and 3D Studio MAX (now Autodesk 3ds Max)

PROFESSIONAL EXPERIENCE

2005–present **SENIOR SOFTWARE ENGINEER**
Telecom International, Raleigh, NC

- Developed reliable, scalable, enterprise-level COM components for customers with thousands of users, using cutting-edge Unified Communications software that supported telephony switches and integrations, including VoIP, T1, analog, and digital. Worked with a complex, multithreaded system.

- Authored technical documents detailing the design and implementation of new voicemail components into the overall system.

- Directed the design and implementation effort to integrate speech recognition into the software using the MRCPv2 protocol.

- Learned multiple telephony technologies, including VoIP and Dialogic TDM. Contributed new features and resolved support issues for related components.

- Created C# testing tools for core application components during development.

- Resolved top-priority support/quality control issues and customer concerns through testing, debugging, and analysis of log files from customer sites.

-continued-

- Collaborated with team members to identify performance improvements for key components and delivered proposals to management; implemented innovative improvements that resulted in better performance gain.

- Worked closely with development partner in Romania, establishing rapport and ongoing communication across differences in time, cultures, and languages.

2002–05 **SENIOR PROGRAMMER ANALYST**
Phoenix Rising Software, Phoenix, AZ

- Built foundation for new graphics engine based on RenderWare, working with artists and designers to ensure flexibility and ease of use for both technical and nontechnical users.

- Wrote tools to streamline work flow and assist team members in creating more accurate and higher-quality products.

- After management decision to add an Xbox version of the product, learned Xbox programming and acted as technical lead for the Xbox platform.

2001–02 **SENIOR PROGRAMMER**
Katsuya, Inc., North America Division, San Jose, CA

- Wrote 3D Studio MAX plug-ins, including exporters, importer, tagging utility, and global utility to manage data shared between plug-ins.

- Created an API based on ODBC to allow programmers to easily retrieve data from a SQL database.

- Developed a unit-testing framework to enable testing of internal libraries.

- Key participant in developing product prototypes and in modernizing and cleaning up proprietary cross-platform libraries.

- Learned Python programming language and collaborated with other programmers to embed it into the game engine.

2000–01 **SENIOR SOFTWARE ENGINEER**
SimuMax, San Jose, CA

- Worked closely with team members to design program architecture for driving simulation software.

- Wrote tools for artists, programmers, and internal departments, including:

  - An exporter plug-in for 3ds Max

  - A tool that allowed artists to tag 3ds Max objects

  - An audio frequency tool for the sound department using DirectMusic

- Designed and wrote the audio and user input systems.

- Responded to artists' needs by quickly learning MAXScript and writing scripts that helped them verify data correctness.

EDUCATION

B.S., Computer Science, San Francisco State University, San Francisco, CA

Julie's hybrid resume easily guides the reader through her twenty years of experience and unique set of skills.

Julie Frisbee Ford, M.A.

998 Timberline Road • El Cerrito, CA 94708
(510) 822-1760 • jfrisbeeford222@sbcglobal.net

Objective

Senior Career Counselor position for a San Francisco Bay Area organization

Highlights of Qualifications

- Twenty years of experience providing career and vocational counseling services to people who reflect the rich diversity found in the Bay Area. In-depth knowledge of Bay Area labor market.

- Extensive experience in developing individual employment plans involving on-the-job training, direct job placement, and educational training, working within strict budget guidelines.

- Negotiated with state agencies and sourced additional funding to ensure success of plans.

- Skillful in building professional and positive relationships with outside vendors, including medical, legal, and educational communities.

Professional Experience

EMPLOYMENT SPECIALIST

Ford and Company, El Cerrito, CA   **1990–present**

- As Case Manager, provided career and vocational counseling to hundreds of displaced workers:
  - Industrially injured workers – Reentry workers – Employees impacted by mass layoffs

- Interviewed clients to assess needs and developed educational strategies for employment plans to meet career development goals.

- Tailored job search plans for clients, with an emphasis on empowering job seekers to manage their own job search. Provided on-the-job training to Job Development staff members.

- Designed and presented workshops and served on panels addressing career planning and job search techniques to local adult schools, colleges, and nonprofit organizations.

- Introduced Job Club concept to the private vocational rehabilitation counseling community.

- Built an in-house resource library of up-to-date materials, including:
  - Bay Area training resources   – Internet access/website referrals
  - Labor market surveys   – Community resources
  - Career development publications   – Employer directories

- Provided clients with information regarding outside resources, such as One Stop Centers, Project Read, Bananas, and ASSETS.

- Became actively involved with legislative issues dealing with injured workers in California.

Evaluation and Assessment

- Conducted interviews and documented personal histories—educational, occupational, avocational—to establish clients' career and vocational needs as well as barriers to employment.

- Administered career development instruments (print and online media) to assist clients with identifying a career focus:
  - Aptitude and academic achievement testing   – CHOICES
  - SkillScan skills assessment   – Self-Directed Search interest instrument
  - Career Values Card Sort   – Strong Interest Inventory

- Monitored and reviewed clients' progress and participation in employment plans to ensure compliance with state laws and regulations. Wrote comprehensive, succinct, and objective case summaries.

Continued on Page 2

Professional Experience, *continued*

Labor Market Research and Analysis

- Conducted hundreds of local labor market surveys, identifying:
  - Job availability
  - Salary ranges
  - Job duties
  - Hiring criteria
  - Physical requirements
  - Labor market trends
- Developed realistic and practical recommendations for a range of career options, incorporating the results of the surveys. Wrote training plans involving, but not limited to, community college programs, extension programs, and local adult schools, always "thinking outside of the box."
- Researched and secured business and community resources to assist with clients' career readjustment.

Administration

- Based on state-mandated budget allotments, researched and calculated individual vocational plan expenditures to best meet program participants' needs while staying within funding constraints.
- Secured financial information from contracted training providers, office supply vendors, ergonomists, and sources of technical support. Years of relationship-building often allowed for negotiation.
- Negotiated with local author to serve as keynote speaker at annual statewide professional conference.
- Published articles in professional association's monthly newsletter: *How to Talk with Your Legislator 101,* and *An Interview with Al Levin,* co-author of *Luck Is No Accident;* contributed to public service brochure produced by the California Association of Rehabilitation and Re-Employment Professionals.
- Tracked and maintained accurate records pertaining to employment plans, including school and outside vendor invoices; reviewed client expenditures and made recommendations for approval.

OUTPLACEMENT COUNSELOR—Subcontractor, Marin General Hospital, Kentfield, CA, 1998

- Participated in rapid response services with hospital employees affected by mass layoff.
- Interviewed employees to assess their most immediate needs and provided referrals to local resources.
- Administered and integrated vocational testing if time allowed.
- Provided employees with individualized, realistic, and doable action plans at end of sessions.

CAREER CENTER ADVISOR—Consultant, Oakland Unified School District, Oakland, CA, 1997

Developed first-ever Career Center in local school serving adult student population.

Education • Affiliations

M.A., Career Development, John F. Kennedy University, Orinda, CA
B.A., Sociology, Syracuse University, Syracuse, NY
CA Adult Education Designated Subjects Teaching Credential, Career Development

• • •

California Association of Rehabilitation and Re-Employment Professionals (CARRP),
Board Member 2002–2006
Small Local Emerging Business (SLEB)—Certified Vendor for the County of Alameda
National Career Development Association (NCDA)

• • •

Computer Skills: Working knowledge of Microsoft Office, email, and Internet

Community Service

Craigslist Foundation Bootcamp, U.C. Berkeley
San Francisco Mayor Gavin Newsom's **Taskforce for the Homeless/Employment Counseling Day**
Job Search Strategies, Merritt College, Oakland, CA
Students and Alumni **Resume critique "Plus" Day,** JFK University, Pleasanton, CA

LORETTA CHANDLER

7827 Eastwick Avenue • Seattle, WA 98133
(206) 375-4288 • lchandler75@yahoo.com

OBJECTIVE

Position as a Research Assistant, Legislative Advocate, or Press Aide for a public policy organization

HIGHLIGHTS OF QUALIFICATIONS

- Creative and thorough, with excellent presentation, written communication, fundraising, and research skills. Strong interest in public policy.
- Documented success in establishing community partnerships, designing effective promotional materials, and generating funding.
- Organized and resourceful, able to work independently and as a team member to complete multiple simultaneous tasks in deadline-driven environments.

RELEVANT EXPERIENCE & ACCOMPLISHMENTS

UNIVERSITY OF CALIFORNIA AT DAVIS, Davis, CA   *Full-time Student*   2008–12

Current Affairs Research Intern, KLAS Public Television, Sacramento, CA   *2010–11*

Assistant Director, ASUCD Student Forums, UC Davis, Davis, CA   *2009–10*

Communication & Research Skills

- Conducted in-depth interviews and extensive print and online research to investigate program topics for *Express* and *MacNeil/Lehrer NewsHour.* Pre-interviewed studio guests. Wrote position papers for *Express* show moderator.
- Negotiated with government and private agencies for data and film footage. Summarized research and prepared informational packets for producers.

Program Development/Media & Publicity

- Collaborated in the planning, promotion, and production of 30 public lectures, with a total audience of 32,000; speakers included author Alice Walker and physicist Edward Teller.
- Corresponded with prospective speakers and scheduled appearance dates. Coordinated and scheduled publicity, organized event logistics, and prepared advertising budget.
- Conceived and produced a comprehensive television program on HIV/AIDS, which aired during community AIDS Awareness Week:
  – Wrote press releases, PSAs, and advertising copy; worked with graphic artists on design of customized promotional materials.
  – Secured media coverage and rebroadcasting of the event on community television.
  – Earned commendations from university administration and the City of Davis.

Fundraising & Community Relations

- Secured funding and support from campus and civic organizations through design and delivery of compelling presentations, meetings with organizational leaders to discuss programming ideas and needs, and successful solicitation of donations of services, including catering, security, and publicity.
- Coordinated and promoted fundraising receptions attended by civic leaders, generating broad media coverage and additional funding.

EDUCATION

B.A., Economics, cum laude, University of California, Davis, CA, 2012

APPENDIX A: ACTION VERBS

These words can help liven up a stale resume. They are grouped under Skill headings, but don't let that stop you from using any that best describe what you need to say.

The underlined words are especially good for pointing out accomplishments.

Management/ Leadership Skills

achieved
administered
analyzed
assigned
attained
chaired
consolidated
contracted
coordinated
delegated
developed
directed
drove
evaluated
executed
expanded
improved
increased
leveraged
mentored
organized
oversaw
pioneered
planned
prioritized
produced
recommended
reduced (losses)
renovated
resolved (problems)

restored
restructured
reviewed
scheduled
spearheaded
strengthened
supervised
tailored

Communication Skills

addressed
arbitrated
arranged
authored
collaborated
convinced
corresponded
developed
directed
drafted
edited
enlisted
formulated
influenced
interpreted
lectured
mediated
moderated
negotiated
persuaded
promoted

publicized
reconciled
recruited
spoke
translated
wrote

Financial Skills

administered
allocated
analyzed
appraised
audited
balanced
budgeted
calculated
computed
developed
forecast
managed
marketed
planned
projected
researched

Teaching Skills

adapted
advised
clarified
coached
communicated
coordinated

demystified
developed
enabled
encouraged
evaluated
explained
facilitated
guided
informed
instructed
persuaded
set goals
stimulated
trained

Technical Skills

assembled
built
calculated
computed
configured
designed
devised
engineered
fabricated
installed
maintained
operated
overhauled
performed
  troubleshooting
programmed

remodeled
repaired
retrieved
solved
upgraded

Research Skills

clarified
collected
critiqued
diagnosed
evaluated
examined
extracted
identified
inspected
interpreted
interviewed
investigated
organized
reviewed
summarized
surveyed
systematized

Clerical or Detail Skills

approved
arranged
catalogued
classified
collected
compiled
executed
generated
implemented
inspected
monitored
operated
organized
prepared
processed
purchased
recorded
retrieved
screened
specified
systematized
tabulated
validated

Helping Skills

assessed
assisted
clarified
coached
counseled
demonstrated
diagnosed
educated
expedited
facilitated
guided
motivated
referred
rehabilitated
represented

Creative Skills

acted
conceived
conceptualized
created
customized
designed
developed

directed
established
fashioned
founded
illustrated
initiated
instituted
integrated
introduced
invented
originated
performed
planned
revitalized
shaped
transformed

APPENDIX B:
INFORMATIONAL INTERVIEWING

"Informational interviewing" is a rather fancy term for a very straightforward, logical, and extremely helpful NETWORKING idea that helps when you are choosing a career field or clarifying your job objective. Here's what you do:

1. Think back on your most enjoyable days of work (or play), and jot down some ideas about what you think you're best at and enjoy doing—not actual job titles, but SKILLS and ABILITIES and TALENTS and INTERESTS—all the things you bring into your various jobs and hobbies.

2. Ask around among all your friends, relatives, friends of relatives, neighbors, people you used to work with (or former boss!), ANYBODY, and get the names of people who are already at work using these same skills and abilities that *you* most enjoy using. Here is where you can *really* make use of different ONLINE SOCIAL NETWORKS like Facebook, Twitter, MySpace, LinkedIn, and others to ask for possible people you could contact to interview for information (*not* for a job—just for information about that line of work).

3. Ask each friend, relative, professional contact, and the like for permission to mention his or her name when you call the person he or she has recommended.

4. Call or email each of the people recommended (or start with an introductory email, and follow up with a phone call—this shows that you are serious and professional), and:
   - Mention the name of the friend or relative or other contact.
   - Ask for fifteen or twenty minutes of the person's time to visit with him or her and learn a bit more about his or her line of work.
   - Explain that you think you might be interested in that field because it uses skills and abilities you have, but you're not sure yet; you're still checking things out and deciding your direction.
   - Tell the contact that you're not looking for a job yet, just getting more information to help you get clear on your job objective.

5. Make an appointment to visit him or her at the workplace for about twenty minutes.

6. Make up a good list of questions that you'd like to ask—for example: How did you get this kind of job? What are the requirements for this work? What are the best and the worst aspects of this work? What kind of pay range can

be expected in this line of work? What chances are there for moving ahead in this field? Ask any question that would help you decide whether this is a good direction for you.

7. Show up right on time for the meeting, ask all your questions, and take some brief notes so you won't forget any of the information.

8. Wrap up the meeting on time, thank the person, and before you leave, ask for the names of TWO OTHER PEOPLE who use those same skills that you want to use in your next job.

9. When you get home, sit down and write that person a short thank-you email and send it right away.

10. The next day, call or email the two people mentioned, make appointments with *them*, and follow the same plan.

11. Continue this process until you find yourself EXCITED and ENTHUSIASTIC about a particular line of work and know that this is the direction you want. Then you'll have a job objective you can happily pursue with all your energy.

12. Always keep in mind that THIS PROCESS WORKS. Although it may *seem* a bit scary, the fact is that people *are* willing to share their information when you show respect for their time, interest in their line of work, and appreciation for their help.

APPENDIX C: SOCIAL NETWORKING

Welcome to the twenty-first century and the digital age! Now, in addition to *or* instead of looking in the newspaper for classified ads, there are tons of job listings you can find online, as well as places to post your resume for employers and recruiters to see. However, it's still the case that many people find new jobs because of their ability to NETWORK—that is, to connect with friends, colleagues, community members, and work acquaintances. More and more, people are connecting with each other **online** through SOCIAL NETWORKS. Social networks bring this networking strategy to the next level, using online resources and websites to expand your network of contacts and therefore your chances of connecting with someone who can help open the door to your next job.

There are networks that help different kinds of individuals and groups to connect, including friends, strangers with common interests, businesses and consumers, scientific researchers, and professionals of all stripes. They also help JOB SEEKERS connect with potential EMPLOYERS and others who might have some helpful advice, provide an **informational interview** (which we've just described in Appendix B), or offer a lead on a possible job opportunity. In addition, more and more employers are using social networks to find top candidates for positions they are looking to fill. Some of the most common social networks that you can join (usually free of charge) are Facebook, Twitter, MySpace, and LinkedIn. In particular, LinkedIn is a professional network that links people who already have jobs, as well as those who *want* jobs.

Whatever field you are interested in, do a little bit of Web research to see whether there is a social or professional network that you can join to find out more about that field, and to connect with people in that line of work. In the case of LinkedIn, you can create a professional profile to let others know what your key strengths are, and you can also post your resume as part of your LinkedIn profile. That way, if employers are looking on LinkedIn for someone with your qualifications, they'll find YOU!

Check out www.damngood.com for the latest information on getting the most out of professional and social networking as part of your job search.

APPENDIX D: CUSTOMIZING YOUR RESUME

Okay, so you've got your resume done, and your Job Objective is Staff Accountant. But wait! A job opportunity comes your way for an Accounting Manager—what to do? The best thing to do is to CUSTOMIZE (or tailor) your resume so that it shows how great you would be as an Accounting Manager.

Here are some tips for customizing your resume:

- Insert the NEW job title into your JOB OBJECTIVE. Do a "Save As" and give your new resume a different file name, so that you can easily distinguish it from any previous resumes. For example, your first resume could be called "Staff Accountant Resume" and the new, customized resume could be named "Accounting Manager Resume."

- Review the job listing for the new job, and highlight any and all of the KEY WORDS AND PHRASES that describe the level and type of experience, special skills, personality traits, training, and education required or preferred, *just as you did in Step 2 originally!*

- Now, check your resume—does it have those key words and phrases in it? Try to insert as many of the new key words and phrases as possible, either within your already existing accomplishment statements, or by adding new statements. In our Accounting example, the Accounting Manager position might require some supervisory or leadership skills and experience. If you have those skills but did not include them on your earlier resume, put them into this new "customized" resume.

- Is there anything on your existing resume that is *not* relevant to the new job opportunity? If so, you can either delete it completely or **change the way you've written it**, so that it is more closely related to your new job goal. For example, in the Staff Accountant resume, you might not want to show your supervisory skills, so you would say: "Collaborated with team members to complete monthly closings." But if you actually did supervise two other staff accountants, then you would change the above statement on your **Accounting Manager resume** to read: "Supervised two Staff Accountants in completing monthly closings."

- Next, take a look at the ORDER of your accomplishment statements. Are they listed in the order that is most impressive and relevant to your **new** target audience? If not, you can rearrange the order of your accomplishment statements— you'd be surprised what a difference that alone can make!

- Remember to **save** your new resume frequently as you revise it. When you have finished customizing, review your new resume carefully to make sure that everything on it *now* is accurate, is spelled correctly, and **looks good.**

>>> **HOT TIP**

Don't worry—it may take you as little as fifteen minutes to customize your resume, and instead of being passed over because your resume didn't show your skills and accomplishments RELEVANT TO THE NEW JOB, you may be called in for an interview!

APPENDIX E: COVER LETTERS AND COVER EMAILS

Your resume should always have a good cover letter attached, as a personal communication between you and the individual who receives the resume.

Many people are intimidated by this task, but it's not that hard if you think of it as just a **friendly, simple communication** from one person (who's looking for a good job) to another (who's looking for a good employee). It is in the interests of both parties to make a good connection!

How to Write a Good Cover Letter

1. **Be sure to address it**—by name and title—**to the person who could hire you.** When it's impossible to learn that person's name, use a functional title, such as "Dear Hiring Manager" or "Dear Human Resources Director." You may have to guess ("Dear Selection Committee"), but *never* say "To whom it may concern" or "Dear Sir or Madam"!

2. **Create a consistent brand identity** by using the same **letterhead**—that is, the way that your name and contact information appear at the top of your resume—for your cover letter. This will give your job search package a consistent, professional look.

3. **Show that you know a little about the company or organization**, that you are aware of their current problems, interests, or priorities.

4. **Express your enthusiasm and interest** in this line of work and this company or organization. Let the employer know what is exciting to you about working for them, and what you "bring to the table." For example, if you have a good idea that might help the employer resolve a problem currently facing their industry, offer to come in and discuss it.

5. **Project warmth and friendliness,** while still being professional. Avoid any generic phrases such as "Enclosed please find . . ." This is a letter to a real live person!

6. **Set yourself apart from the crowd.** Identify at least one thing about you that's unique—say, a special talent for getting along with everybody at work or some unusual skill that goes beyond the essential requirements of the position— something that distinguishes you *and* is relevant to the job. (Then, if several others are equally qualified for the job, your uniqueness may be the reason to choose YOU.)

7. **Be specific** about what you are asking for and what you are offering. Make it clear which position you're applying for and the specific experience or skills you have that relate to that position.

8. **Take the initiative** about the next step whenever possible, and again, be specific. "I'll call your office early next week to see when we could meet to discuss this job opening," for example. *Or*—if you're exploring for unannounced jobs that may come up—"I'll call your office next week to set up a time to discuss your company's needs for help in the near future."

9. **Keep it brief**—a few short paragraphs, all on one page.

Sample Cover Letters

The following are sample cover letters from *real people* whose resumes also appear in the Sample Resumes section of this book. The date and the job seeker's letterhead have been removed to save space.

SEE BEVERLY'S RESUME ON PAGE 46.

Hiring Manager
Farnsworth, Smythe and Mattel, LLP
2167 Oak Street, 4th Floor
Cincinnati, OH 53536

Re: Administrative Assistant—Law Firm position

Dear Hiring Manager:

I was excited to find your recent listing for the above position, and to discover how well it matches my skills, experience, and career goals. I have attached my resume for your review and consideration.

During my tenure at Stein, Falcon & Morgan, I held a dual role: As Recruiting Coordinator, I provided comprehensive assistance in managing the Fall On-Campus Recruiting and Summer Internship programs. As Administrative Assistant, I provided administrative support to the attorneys, including travel coordination, expense tracking, and any additional tasks or projects that were needed.

I took a hiatus from the legal field in order to raise my children, and applied my energy and attention to support local schools as Chair of multiple committees and also as a Sales Associate at Nordstrom, all of which have kept my administrative, teamwork, and client relationship-building skills honed.

I am now ready and eager to return to the rigors and dynamic environment of a law firm. I would welcome the opportunity to apply my drive, experience, and unique combination of skills to support the Attorney Recruiting and Professional Development functions as an Administrative Assistant at Farnsworth, Smythe and Mattel.

I would be happy to speak with you directly to further discuss the requirements of the position, salary, and any questions you may have regarding my qualifications.

Thank you for your consideration. I look forward to hearing from you in the near future.

Sincerely,
Beverly Hamilton

Attachment: Resume

Coordinator of Personnel
Lincoln High School
938 Missouri Boulevard
Minneapolis, MN 59727

Dear Coordinator:

I was very pleased to learn of the opening for the position of Principal at your high school.

In my enclosed resume I have outlined my professional and educational background and given special attention to those experiences and accomplishments that address your school's stated needs and requirements.

I am a "take charge" type of administrator and have demonstrated strong leadership and initiative in addressing the most difficult problems at a number of schools. I have a particularly strong record of success in developing curricula that meet the needs of all students.

It is my nature and philosophy to look for the best in students and to do whatever is necessary to help them perform to their fullest potential. With this in mind, I recently attended a workshop at Harvard University (and plan to return this summer), where materials have been developed to effectively teach study skills to high school students with diverse learning styles. This workshop prepared me to introduce these critically important materials to teachers for use in their classrooms.

I would welcome the opportunity to share with you additional examples of contributions I might make to the program at your school, and I will call later this week to see if we can arrange an appointment.

Sincerely,
Ruben Saragossa

Enclosure: Resume

>>> Because Ruben only recently completed the Harvard University workshop, he did not include it in his resume; however, including the information about the workshop in his *cover letter* further strengthened Ruben's job search package. SEE RUBEN'S RESUME ON PAGE 54.

Stacey is aware that, while some companies offer relocation packages as part of the hiring process, many do not have the funds to do so. By including the "P.S." in her cover letter, Stacey is letting the consulting firm know that they will not need to pay for her to move to Denver. In this way, she strengthens her position and lets them know that she should be taken seriously as a qualified candidate. SEE STACEY'S RESUME ON PAGE 34.

Human Resources Director
Ellsworth Consulting
1517 Broad Street
Denver, CO 83702

Re: Executive/Personal Assistant positions

Dear Human Resources Director:

With more than fifteen years of experience as both an Executive Assistant and a Personal Assistant, I was excited to find your recent listings in the Denver area. I am currently in the process of relocating to Colorado and would welcome the opportunity to speak with you further about these opportunities. I have attached my resume for your review.

During my career, I have worked with many types of executives, from the most particular to the most relaxed. I have provided outstanding, precise, and accurate administrative support to business executives in diverse industries and in deadline-driven, global business environments. I have consistently received stellar references from my employers, several of whom are recognized financial services and investment leaders.

Although I have not completed a four-year degree, my professional history has enabled me to acquire and use all of the skills and expertise necessary to be an outstanding EA/Personal Assistant. I would be happy to provide you with a list of references at your convenience.

I would appreciate the opportunity to speak with you about your EA and Personal Assistant openings in Denver and vicinity, and to further discuss how my qualifications are an excellent match for your needs.

Thank you for your consideration. I look forward to hearing from you in the very near future.

Sincerely,
Stacey Carmichael

Attachment: Resume

P.S. As I am already in the process of relocating, I will not require a relocation package in order to secure a position in the Denver area.

SEE MARIA'S RESUME ON PAGE 40.

Marjorie Lawrence, Director
Professional Training Institute
3482 Elmwood Lane
Philadelphia, PA 19710

Dear Ms. Lawrence,

The position of Marketing Trainer that you described in our recent conversation is an opportunity of great motivational and professional dimensions. I can envision a strong team atmosphere, working to achieve the Institute's goals, with an emphasis on commitment to the representatives' growth potential.

My attached resume will show that I have a strong training background. I have a great deal to contribute to the department, given my experience and interest, as well as my sense of humor and creative energy.

I am very excited about the position. The people, functions, and environment all add up to a very appealing challenge. I look forward to talking with you in person.

Sincerely,
Maria Benjamin

Attachment: Resume

Cover Emails

When you are emailing your resume to an employer, you may want to (or be required to) attach a complete cover letter along with your resume. In some cases, however, you may simply want to write a brief *cover email*. The same basic principles that apply to writing a cover letter also apply to a cover email, but a cover email is even more brief and to the point. Additional differences include:

1. A cover email does not include your letterhead or the address of the business you are sending to.

2. On the Subject line, be clear (and brief!) about the position you are applying for.

3. Just type your name at the end of the cover email; do *not* include any online signature you may have established.

4. Remember to attach your resume! Use the program or format that is requested by the employer—such as Microsoft Word (.doc or .docx), plain text (.txt), or Photoshop (.pdf).

5. Remember to send a "blind copy" (bcc) to yourself, so that when you receive it, that should mean (although it's no fool-proof guarantee) that your resume was, in fact, also sent to the employer.

Sample Cover Emails

The following are sample cover emails of job seekers whose resumes also appear in the Sample Resumes section of this book. You can see how cover emails are shorter than cover letters, and that the job seeker also sent a blind copy (bcc) to him- or herself. These are also written in Arial, the font most often used for sending emails.

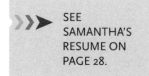

SEE SAMANTHA'S RESUME ON PAGE 28.

To: humanresourcesdirector@serenitasmedicalcenter.org
Bcc: samanthabjensen@gmail.com
Subject: Certified Nursing Assistant position at Serenitas Medical Center

Dear Human Resources Director:

As a recent graduate of the Certified Nursing Assistant program at Vermont College of Science & Technology, I am excited about beginning my new career as a CNA in the Brattleboro area. I was pleased to find your recent listing online, and I have attached my resume for your consideration.

I have also completed my Acute Care Certification and was glad to find that Serenitas is not only home to a regional Trauma Center but also offers a wide range of rehabilitation services.

I would welcome the opportunity to speak with you further about how I might best support Serenitas Medical Center in improving the health of individuals and communities.

Thank you very much. I look forward to hearing from you soon.

Sincerely,
Samantha Jensen

Attachment: Resume

SEE DAVID'S RESUME ON PAGE 50.

To: hiringmanager@GoldToothWirelessSolutions.com
Bcc: chengdavidb@gmail.com
Subject: Help Desk Manager position

Dear Hiring Manager:

Thank you for contacting me about the Help Desk Manager position. As I may have mentioned in our conversation, I have more than 15 years of leadership in IT operations and management at UPS. I am now ready to use my skills in a new, fast-growing IT service organization. My resume is attached.

I would appreciate the opportunity to meet with you to further discuss the details of my resume, and how I might best support the vision and goals of GoldTooth Wireless Solutions as the Help Desk Manager.

Thank you for your consideration. I look forward to our meeting.

Sincerely,
David B. Cheng

INDEX

DAMN GOOD JOB SEARCH HELP

RESUME WRITING SERVICE. From anywhere in the world, get your resume written by The Damn Good Resume Team. A professional resume writer will compose and produce your resume, working with you by phone, fax, or email. If you live in the San Francisco area, you can get your resume written during an in-person session.

RESUME CRITIQUE SERVICE. If you've already written your resume, use The Damn Good Resume Critique Service to make sure you have the most effective job search tool possible. A professional resume writer will examine your resume and give you a half-hour critique by phone. (Believe me, we pack a lot of information into a half-hour session!)

CAREER COUNSELING. If you're having trouble figuring out how to proceed in your existing career or how to make a career change, get advice from a professional counselor. A skilled career counselor can help you define your talents, understand how to optimize them in your career, and create long- and short-term career plans. If you live in the San Francisco area, meet in person with a counselor on The Damn Good Job Search Team. Counseling services are also provided by phone and email.

JOB SEARCH COACHING. Do you feel overwhelmed with the prospect of finding and winning a job? Get help from a career coach on The Damn Good Job Search Team. She'll help you develop your job hunt strategy and motivate you through the process of conducting your job market research, cold calling, interview preparation, effective follow-up, and salary negotiations. If you live in the San Francisco area, work with a career coach in person or in a group that's facilitated by a professional coach. Individual coaching sessions are also conducted by phone.

READY-MADE RESUMES. Need help writing your resume on your own? This online resume builder has 150 professional resume templates, 800 copy-and-paste resume phrases, and lots of resume samples. Extra bonus: Ready-Made Cover Letters: templates for cover letters, cover emails, follow-ups to recruiters, website cover notes, and thank-you letters. These are the same tools used by professional resume writers.

Find all of these Damn Good services and products at:

www.damngood.com